WTF?
COLLEGE

How to Survive 101 of Campus's
Worst F*#!-ing Situations

GREGORY BERGMAN AND JODI MILLER

adamsmedia

Avon, Massachusetts

Published by Adams Media,
a division of F+W Media, Inc.
57 Littlefield Street, Avon, MA 02322. U.S.A.
www.adamsmedia.com

ISBN 10: 1-4405-0035-5
ISBN 13: 978-1-4405-0035-0

Printed in the United States of America.

J I H G F E D C B

Library of Congress Cataloging-in-Publication Data is available from the publisher.

This publication is designed to provide accurate and authoritative information with regard
to the subject matter covered. It is sold with the understanding that the publisher is not
engaged in rendering legal, accounting, or other professional advice. If legal advice or
other expert assistance is required, the services of a competent professional person
should be sought.

> —From a *Declaration of Principles* jointly adopted by a Committee of the
> American Bar Association and a Committee of Publishers and Associations

Many of the designations used by manufacturers and sellers to distinguish their product
are claimed as trademarks. Where those designations appear in this book and Adams
Media was aware of a trademark claim, the designations have been printed with initial
capital letters.

Certain sections of this book deal with activities and devices that would be in violation
of various federal, state, and local laws if actually carried out or constructed. We do not
advocate the breaking of any law. This information is for entertainment purposes only.
We recommend that you contact your local law enforcement officials before undertaking
any project based upon any information obtained from this book. We are not responsible
for, nor do we assume any liability for, damages resulting from the use of any information in this book.

This book is available at quantity discounts for bulk purchases.
For information, please call 1-800-289-0963.

This is dedicated to all the girls who
get through college by getting wasted
and whoring themselves.—GB

This is dedicated to my parents who
said that getting wasted and whoring
myself through college would never
get me anywhere.—JM

contents

Introduction

Welcome to F*#!-ing College

WTF? is back. And this time we are here to help our friends in college, university, or for the mentally or financially challenged among you—community college. In this book, we've compiled 101 of the worst fucking situations you'll experience in collegiate life and our recommendations on how to survive them.

When you were a little kid, adults told you that those were the "best days of your life." *Their reasoning:* You didn't have to do shit for yourself and you had no responsibilities. *Translation:* You don't have to deal with a pain-in-the-ass kid like you.

But the truth is that they were lying. Kid life, like adult life, sucks. While kids don't have to pay the bills, they do have to obey the people who do. But not anymore. In college, you now have the best of both worlds; you have limited responsibility and no one to boss you around. These really are the "best days of your life." After all, bagging a new hottie every night in real life requires more than fetching a cup of lukewarm beer from a keg and showing off your calf muscles. Trust us.

Indeed, college is a great time in life. It is a time to learn, to grow, and to participate in sexually deviant behavior with random coeds without the fear of your mom walking in. It is the peak of your existence, the time when your mind and body are at their very best.

We, your humble authors, remember our college experience fondly:

"I drank a lot and did a lot of drugs and learned some stuff that I mostly forgot," says coauthor Gregory Bergman on the subject. Mr. Bergman is the proud recipient of a BA in Philosophy, which left him forever critical of so-called "reality" as well as utterly unemployable in the "real" world.

"I drank a lot and did a lot of drugs too, but I don't really think I learned that much to be honest," adds co-author Jodi Miller. Ms. Miller is the proud recipient of a BA in Media Communications and Broadcast Journalism (a bullshit degree by the way—you might want to look into it!), which has left

her nothing but a phony smile and distant memories of what it was like to not be old.

Yep, it's all downhill from college. Again, you'll have to trust us.

But that doesn't mean college is a breeze. To master this new chapter in your life, you must learn to avoid the potential pitfalls and navigate the tough situations that come your way—situations that range from sleeping through a final exam to knocking up your professor to coping with a harrowing weed addiction. How do you learn to deal with these and other tough situations?

You read this book, you freshman dumbass. WTF?

Chapter 1

Orientation

1. You Applied to Twenty Schools— and Were Only Accepted at One

Choosing a college can be a very difficult decision. Does it have a good reputation? Is it expensive? Do the chicks there put out? But for you it's even harder. Truth is your grades aren't perfect, so you apply to twenty schools just in case. Surely you'll get accepted to at least ten or so. But soon the thin envelopes start to arrive. *Rejected. Rejected. Rejected.* And yet another goddamn *rejected!* You have been turned down from every school you applied to except one. One! You are now the newest student at Loser University. WTF?

The WTF Approach to Handling F*#!-ing Rejections

► OPTION #1: *Make the Most of It*

So what if the school's motto is "We're a bunch of rejects, but we are really nice . . . and stuff." And who cares if the campus is old and dirty and the computer room looks like something out of a 1950s sci-fi film. Look on the bright side: Your professors probably grade on one hell of a curve.

► OPTION #2: *Transfer*

Get good grades the first semester and then get the fuck out of Dodge. Some slightly less shitty school might accept you now.

► **OPTION #3: *Stay Home with Mom and Dad***

Fuck it. Get a job at Dairy Queen instead. Maybe you can work your way up to assistant manager or even manager one day. That's when the *big* bucks start rolling in.

EXCERPTS FROM RECENTLY DISCOVERED COLLEGE ESSAYS:

"I am a hard worker and true team player. I enjoy football, golf, and just about any type of physical activity that is hands-on. Above all, I consider family to be the most important thing."

> OJ Simpson
> Intended Major: *Forensic Science*

"I have a lot of leadership skills. People tend to trust that I know the final solution to even the most tedious of problems."

> Adolf Hitler
> Intended Major: *Jewish Studies, with a minor in Art*

"I believe in turning the other cheek, not coveting thy neighbor's wife, and that the meek shall inherit the earth. I think one day people all over the world will cherish these principles—to such an extent that they will kill, maim, and torture those who do not."

> Jesus H. Christ
> Intended Major: *Religious Studies*

"I like to grill hamburgers and hit people."

> George Foreman
> Intended Major: *Sports Medicine, with a minor in Culinary Arts*

"I am a true visionary, the kind you'll one day read about in history books. I enjoy writing, playing 'conspiracy against the King' with my pals, and having sexual relations with our many slaves."

> Thomas Jefferson
> Intended Major: *Government*

"My neighbor's dog told me I should apply to your school. You should really consider accepting me. Seriously."

> David Berkowitz
> a.k.a. Son of Sam
> Intended Major: *Abnormal Psychology*

"I will get into your school—by any means necessary."

> Malcom X
> Intended Major: *African-American Studies*

"I have always believed that it is important both in school and in life to 'back that ass up' when appropriate."

> Terius Gray a.k.a. Juvenile
> Intended Major: *Undecided, but mostly just going to chill and smoke weed*

"My grades aren't so good, but I have an enormous cock."

> John Holmes
> Intended Major: *Sexual Education*

"My last name is Bush, as in, the son of George Herbert Walker Bush. See you at school! The End."

> George W. Bush
> Intended Major: *Undecided, and honestly not really planning to try that hard. Did I mention my last name?*

IN THE FUTURE

Apply to fifty schools instead of twenty. Or, don't be a loser in the first place.

2. You Only Got In Because of Your Dad's Donations

Poor little rich boy. You didn't mind that Daddy threw some money around so you could wind up in the Ivy League rather than community college—and forgot all about the cash he sent you to pimp out your dorm room—but now you're pissed. Everyone's making fun of you because they know the only reason you're here is that your dad donated a ton of cash to the school.

The WTF Approach to Handling Your F*#!-ing Legacy Issues

➤ OPTION #1: *Change Your Name*

Chances are, if your dad's a campus big shot, there's some building or fund named after him. If you change your name, no one will know that you're related. Pick a cool, single-word name like Prince, Cher, or Madonna—realizing that you're obviously gay if you listen to any of them.

NOTE: This is more important if you have a unique last name such as O'Gubersteinsmith or something. If the Stern School of Business at NYU is named after your dad, it's not likely anyone will make the connection just because your last name is Stern. There are probably a few more Sterns there—and Steinbergs and Goldbergs and, well, you get the picture.

➤ OPTION #2: *Beat Your Dad*

It may not be easy growing up in the shadow of a great man, but it is possible to outdo even your legendary pop. Many sons in history have outclassed and out-succeeded their big-shot fathers. For example, George H.W. Bush was a shitty president for only four years, while his son was twice as shitty a president for twice as long.

➤ OPTION #3: *Use It to Get Laid*

So what if you're a dumb ass and your daddy paid your way into school? When you're getting your rocks off with a hot chick in your dorm room because of your last name, you might not care so much that the building you're screwing in is named after Dad.

➤ OPTION #4: *Kill Daddy*

Time to put that Freud stuff you learned in psychology class to good use. Kill your father and end his evil reign over your soul just like Sigmund's theory of the Oedipus complex says every son wants to do.

> **PROFESSOR TIP:** Banging your mother, however, is ill advised. But it is always an option if you're experiencing a dry spell.

YOUR DAD MAY BE BETTER THAN YOU IF . . .

❑ His penis is *still* bigger than yours.
❑ He knows more about fly-fishing than you.
❑ He's more proficient with a carving knife on Thanksgiving.
❑ He can still beat your ass.
❑ Your girlfriend chooses to have sex with him over you.

Quit Your Bitching

There are worse last names and worse legacies than yours. How'd you like to show up to school with a last name like . . .

● Dahmer
● Manson
● Hitler
● Bush

3. All the Housing on Campus Is Full

It's your first day of college. You made it. You can barely contain your excitement. But when you go to check in, you find out there's been some sort of mix up and your room has boon givon to another student—and thoro aro no moro available rooms. How's that for a welcome?

The WTF Approach to Finding Some F*#!-ing Housing

➤ OPTION #1: *Live with a Family Losing Their Home*

These dire economic times have put many families on the verge of becoming homeless. They'll take you in for a few bucks to help pay the mortgage.

➤ OPTION #2: *Couch Surf*

Be that loser guy who's always crashing on someone's sofa. Work out some payment arrangement— be it grass, booze, or cash—and someone will surely let you in.

➤ OPTION #3: *Become a Gigolo*

Find a different girl to hook up with every night and just stay at her place.

➤ OPTION #4: *Become a Squatter*

Live in an abandoned building with some punk-rock dirtbags. Be prepared to dress the part: Spend many hours trying desperately to look like shit.

4. You Are the Only White Kid on Campus

You thought the brochure included a lot of minorities in the photos in order to be politically correct. Like every advertisement, it showed the classic four: one Asian, one black, one nondescript dark-haired person that is supposed to be Latino, and then one white fool like you. What they neglected to tell you, however, was that you would be the *only* white fool.

The WTF Approach to Flying F*#!-ing Solo

➤ STEP #1: *Constantly Apologize*

Keep saying you are sorry over and over again and take personal responsibility for the actions of all white men who lived before you.

➤ STEP #2: *Use a lot of Hyphens*

Remember, the term is "African-American" not "black," "Asian-American" not "Chinese," and "Arab-American" not "terrorist."

➤ STEP #3: *Say You Are Part Cherokee*

Everyone claims to be part Cherokee. This will at least give you a little minority cred.

➤ STEP #4: *Use Your Whiteness to Your Advantage*

How often do you get to be exotic anyhow? In Nebraska you were just another blond, blue-eyed, corn-fed dummy, but here you're the *only* blond, blue-eyed, corn-fed dummy—you're going to be a hit.

➤ STEP #5: *Act Black*

Sometimes if white kids act black enough for a long enough time, it's considered acceptable to the black community. Think Eminem.

The Jew of Howard U

You can get into a more prestigious college if you are willing to be the odd man out. Just as quotas can benefit minorities, they can also benefit white kids. A friend of ours screwed up his LSATs and didn't get into the law schools of his choice. So he looked to Howard University, which was a better school than the ones that *did* accept him. Not only did he end up getting admitted, he got a scholarship. Why? Because he was a white Orthodox Jew.

So be smart and don't be afraid to be the minority. After all, how do you think they feel half the time, you insensitive white asshole?

Stuff White People Used *to Like*

You've probably heard of the popular book, *Stuff White People Like*, which is a collection of different things that tickle white peoples' fancy, but what about the stuff white people *used* to like? Here's a list of some of the stuff that white people used to really get a kick out of:

- Mercantilism
- Jousting
- Powdered wigs
- Snuff
- Masques
- Crusades
- Colonization
- Killing witches
- The slave trade

5. You Are the Only Black Kid on Campus

White boys, white boys, and *more* white boys—goddamn, this school looks like a Green Day concert. And then of course there's a sampling of Asians, Latinos, and a bunch of foreigners from who knows where. But as for black folk? None—besides you.

The WTF Approach to Handling a Lack of F#*!-ing Diversity

> **OPTION #1: *Be a Soul-less Man***

Remember the movie *Soul Man* about the white guy who downs a bunch of "bronzing pills" to turn himself "black" and get a scholarship to Harvard? He learned a lot about himself and about race relations during his little experiment. Do the same, but become white. Find out what skin-whitening pills Michael Jackson takes and do the same. You may lose a little soul, but at least you'll develop a new appreciation for country music, tuna on white bread with extra mayo, and Starbucks Frappuccinos. Yummy!

> **OPTION #2: *Embrace It***

Shit, do you know how many white girls will want to sleep with you? But only if you play your cards right—and fill every stereotype these lily-white college chicks lust after. If you can't rap, buy a karaoke machine and practice; if you can't dance, hit the clubs and improve your groove; if you can't play basketball . . . wait, that's ridiculous, *of course* you can play basketball.

➤ OPTION #3: *Recruit*

Call up your boys at home and encourage them to transfer to your school. Explain Option #2 to them. Then start a fraternity and bang every chick in school.

➤ OPTION #4: *Scare People*

You might as well use your unique blackness to get back at Whitey. Wear all black with a black beret, like the Black Panthers. Instead of raising your hand in class, make a tight fist and raise your arm in one powerful motion.

COLLEGE KID QUOTE

"I went to a school where there were only two and a half black students. Me and a pregnant girl."

—Ted Codington,
junior at Davidson College

➤ OPTION #5: *Transfer*

If you *really* can't handle it, transfer to a school that isn't so white bread. After you switch schools, write a book about your experiences at the all-white school, and send it to Oprah.

WTFACT: In 1962, James Meredith became the first black student enrolled at the University of Mississippi. He was escorted in by U.S. marshals on his first day of class.

6. Your Mom's Calling Everyday Because She Misses You

The beeping, the vibrating, the flashing light on your phone—to the average eye it looks like you're really popular. You're always blowing up with calls and texts. But what no else knows, and you pray they never find out, is that nine out of the last ten missed calls were from Mom. Yep, her little boy has gone off to college and she misses you. Aren't you glad you suggested that unlimited calling plan?

The WTF Approach to Dealing with a F*#!-ing Helicopter Parent

➤ OPTION #1: *Lay Down the Law*

Explain to her that this is part of life and she knew this day would come. Tell her you love her and you miss her, too (even if it's not true), but that you cannot grow as a person if your mommy keeps calling. Then set a calling schedule so you can set aside time between partying and eating pizza to catch up.

> OPTION #2: *Change Your Number*

If she's not paying for your cell phone bill, then you have every right to go off the grid. If the only benefit you get from Mom is an overcooked turkey on Thanksgiving or a bad Christmas sweater, cut the cord and don't look back.

> OPTION #3: *Use It to Your Advantage*

People like a popular guy. Change the name in your phone from Mom to something like Candy or Daisy, then whenever a call or text comes in, your friends will just think you've got a stalker.

NOTE: If your mom's name is really Candy or Daisy, be thankful you made it to college.

> OPTION #4: *Get Her Laid*

If your mom has been single for a while, it's no wonder she's holding on to you so tightly. Find her a man to take the edge off. If the sex is really good, you might never hear from her again.

Is Your Mom a MILF?

This might not be a bad thing. Have her come up and party with you instead of chat on the phone. It could make you very popular.

YOUR MOM IS A MILF IF . . .

❏ When she takes off her bra, her tits don't touch her belly button.
❏ Everyone thinks she's your older sister.
❏ When she leaves the house in a mini-skirt she stops traffic—in a good way.
❏ Even *you* tried to screw her once

7. You Call Your Mom Everyday Because You Miss Her

You couldn't wait to leave home and be on your own. You can eat what you want, wear what you want, stay out as late as you want. You can get drunk in the afternoon and dance naked until you vomit all over your room if you want. You were *so* ready for all of that. But what you weren't ready for was this strange aching in your belly whenever you think about home. Turns out you are really homesick and missing your mommy. Pussy!

The WTF Approach to Stop Being Such a F*#!-ing Mama's Boy

➤ OPTION #1: *Find a Replacement*

Date a girl who reminds you of Mom. Not looks-wise, sicko. Find yourself a girl who likes to take care of you the way Mom does, like make you soup when you're sick, do your laundry, and pay for your shit. When you get over that homesick feeling, dump her ass and find yourself a raging bitch . . . they're more fun.

➤ OPTION #2: *Numb Yourself*

Get drunk and stay drunk. Yeah you'll probably become an alcoholic, but at least you won't be a mama's boy.

➤ OPTION #3: *Spend the Weekend with Mom*

Chances are, by Sunday you'll remember all the reasons why you wanted to go away to school in the first place.

➤ OPTION #4: *Drop Out and Move Home*

If you really can't take the separation any longer, transfer to a school that is closer to home and commute—like the pathetic loser that you are.

Yo Mama So . . .

Everyone remembers this classic schoolyard slam. Here are some favorites:

- Yo mama so fat she goes to a restaurant, looks at the menu, and says, "Okay!"
- Yo mama so stupid it took her two hours to watch *60 Minutes*.
- Yo mama so greasy she sweats Crisco!
- Yo mama so poor her face is on the front of a food stamp.
- Yo mama so nasty that she pours salt water down her pants to keep her crabs fresh.

Are You Too Close to Your Mom?

You could be too close to your mom. Here are the top three signs that your relationship is a little too intimate.

1. She breastfed you until the end of the seventh grade.
2. The thought of her home-made apple pie makes you cream.
3. When she asks if you "want seconds," she's referring to intercourse.

8. You Run Up Your Credit Card on Non-Emergency Things

When your parents gave you a credit card to take to college they told you it was to be used explicitly for school supplies and emergencies. But when your dad gets the latest statement, he has a hard time believing that case of beer, a leather jacket, and the Wii console were *real* emergencies. In fact, you somehow managed to rack up over $2,000 in debt. WTF are you going to say?

The WTF Approach to Beating F*#!-ing Charges

> **OPTION #1: *Report It Stolen***

It happens all the time. People steal credit cards and charge the shit out of them. Tell your parents that you lost your wallet at a frat party a while ago and when you got it back, you didn't even think to look for the card because you rarely use it. Remember, you're the victim here.

> **OPTION #2: *Flip the Switch***

Explain to your parents that you don't agree with their definition of "emergency." It must be a generational thing. You were only trying to fit in at school by buying cool stuff like everyone else. Peer pressure is a nasty thing. Tell them they should be thankful that you didn't turn to drugs.

➤ OPTION #3: *Fess Up*

Apologize and tell them the temptation was too great. Then promise to pay them back once you graduate and get a real job. By the time that happens, they'll be dead. Win-win. Well, not for them . . . so more of just a win, really.

WTFACT: When using your parents' credit card, buy beer and food at gas stations. The bill will only state the name of the gas station and not the items you purchase. This way you can claim that you were only buying gas. You're welcome, scumbag.

PROFESSOR TIP: Word to the wise: It's kind of suspicious to claim that you spent $100 on gas unless you're filling up a semi.

9. There's a Blackout on Campus During Your Study Session

You're in the middle of "studying"—playing video games and occasionally glancing at your closed book—when everything goes black. No lights, no television, nothing. At first you think you blew a fuse, but when you look out into the hall you realize it's the whole dorm. Then you look out your window and it's the whole campus. Damn.

The WTF Approach to Dealing with No F*#!-ing Electricity

➤ STEP #1: *Loot the School*

If you need some extra cash, get a couple friends together and start looting. Dress in black and hit the computer labs, video departments, and anywhere else with expensive equipment.

➤ STEP #2: *Engage in* Frotteurism

A *frotteur*—for those of you who have yet to take Psych 101—gets off by rubbing himself against others in public places. Use the cover of night to surreptitiously rub against whomever you fancy. Good times.

➤ STEP #3: *Black Out!*

The lights are off and the power's out. Finish up your night of mayhem by throwing a party and getting so wasted that you black out. Get it, black out and *blackout*? In other words, do the same as you would any other night, just with the lights off.

What Not to Do

Cry like a bitch. If you are still afraid of the dark, then you're probably crying like the pathetic little piece of crap that you are. Call your mommy on your cell and then read Entry #7: You Call Your Mom Everyday Because *You* Miss *Her* (page 14)—you'll need the help, baby.

(page 14)

WTFACT: One of the worst blackouts in U.S. history was the New York City blackout of 1977. The blackout lasted over twenty-four hours and resulted in massive looting and arson. In all, 1,616 stores were damaged, 1,037 fires were called in, and 3,776 people were arrested. Estimated cost of damages amounted to a little over $300 million—which, incidentally, is the current median price for a one-bedroom condo in Manhattan.

10. Your Ride Home for the Holidays Ditches You

The air is getting cold, holiday lights and decorations are everywhere, and the spirit of the season has slowly begun to warm even your cold, black heart. You have been looking forward to this time off to spend with your family for a while. But a few days before you are about to leave for the holidays, your ride leaves without you.

The WTF Approach to Getting F*#!-ing Home

➤ OPTION #1: *Go Greyhound*

Unlike the airlines, some bus companies offer special deals around the holidays for losers, so it shouldn't cost you too much. While it might take longer and smell worse than a plane, you'll get there eventually.

➤ OPTION #2: *Hitchhike*

Hitching a ride is a great way to see the country and possibly learn something about yourself. Bring a copy of Kerouac's *On the Road* and pretend that what you are doing is romantic. Make sure to jot your experiences down too. While your collection of stories might not end up as well-written or insightful as Kerouac's, in today's more dangerous world it might be more exciting—especially the part about you escaping from being held as a sex slave in the belly of a semitrailer driven by a bisexual born-again Christian ex-con named Billy Bob.

➤ OPTION #3: *Steal a Car*

Wait until about 1 A.M. then take off. By the time the owner realizes his car's gone you could be home. Tell your parents it's a friend's car. Then when you return to campus, leave it in a ditch. The cops will find it and return it to the owner. He'll be happy the car is in the same shape it was before—minus those few hundred extra miles.

COLLEGE KID QUOTE

"My mommy and daddy don't love me enough to pay my way home. I hate my life and I hate the holidays and I want to die."

—Jacob Stein, law student at University of Chicago

IN THE FUTURE

Be born to better parents who love you and won't strand you at school.

➤ OPTION #4: *Stay at School*

While the school will be pretty empty, the students who stay behind are just as depressed as you and want to forget their holiday gloom. So throw a party and get wasted. Remember, the only girls who are still at school during Christmas are filthy whores who were disowned by their parents a long time ago.

11. You Can't Lose the Freshman Fifteen

Welcome to real life, prick! You think you can just eat like a pig and drink beer all day and not gain weight for the rest of your life? Well, you can't. Those days are over, pal. Time to cut down on Dominos and do some friggin' exercise. *Capiche?* You'd know what that meant if you weren't failing Italian, fat boy.

The WTF Approach to Shedding the F*#!-ing Pounds

▶ STEP #1: *Stop Drinking Beer*

I know it sounds insane, but you can do it. Switch to drinking pure vodka or, if you're a pussy, Bacardi and Diet Coke. You'll get just as wasted but you'll stay slim.

▶ STEP #2: *Vomit Yourself Thin*

You'll be the only bulimic guy in your frat. Won't that be cool? You will be so trendy, like a model.

▶ STEP # 3: *Shit Yourself Thin*

Go one step further than becoming bulimic to really see the pounds shed. If you shit more, then you'll have less food inside you, which will make you skinnier. Take lots of laxatives every morning before class. Make sure to wear dark jeans in case you crap yourself. Yummy.

►STEP #4: *Screw Yourself Thin*

Hopefully after Steps #1–3, you're a little less chubby than before, and you can actually find a chick who *wants* to bang your fat ass. Now you just need to get laid more. Think of it this way: If you have more sex, then you will lose more weight, and therefore you will become more appealing, which in turn allows you to have even more sex. That's Logic 101, biatch.

NOTE: The skinnier you get, the bigger your dick looks!

for the ladies . . .

Just go with it and become a fat slut. If you have already gained fifteen pounds it's probably due to drinking beer, which means that you're getting wasted a lot, which means that you are probably already getting your fair share of dick. That's Logic 101, biatch.

NOTE: The fatter you get, the bigger your tits get!

WHAT THE F*#! IS UP WITH . . .
BLAMING A
"BAD METABOLISM"

Listen up, fat America: bad metabolism, *shmad* metabolism. If you eat a lot and don't move, you get fat. Simple. So don't give us that metabolism nonsense—just get the Krispy Kreme out of your mouth and hit the gym, fat ass.

Diets to Beat the Fifteen

Following are some new diets that you might want to try:

Rock diet: Eat rocks. They're cheap, plentiful, and very low-calorie.

Rock cocaine diet: Smoke crack and you'll never be hungry again.

French diet: Nobody knows how they stay so skinny with all of their fatty foods, but somehow they pull it off. Warning: Side effects include spontaneous cowardice, rapid armpit hair growth, and overall ennui.

Sushi diet: Avoid the tempura and just stick to raw fish and you'll be slim in no time. Warning: Side effects include spontaneously breaking out into karaoke, dressing like an anime character, and radiation poisoning.

Endangered species diet: Because they're illegal to kill and hard to find, dinner is going to be difficult. That said, until you've had a bald eagle sandwich you just haven't lived.

IN THE FUTURE . . .

Be that overconfident, beer-belly college guy. You know, the guy at the party that's the loudest and most obnoxious and is convinced that every girl wants him? Be him. He gets laid despite his belly—and doesn't have to deal with any of that exercise bullshit.

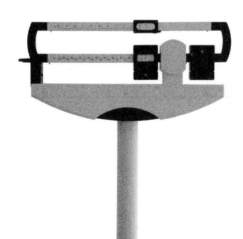

12. You Don't Receive as Much Financial Aid as You Expected

You somehow managed to survive your first year of school despite spending the majority of your school loan money on party expenses like plastic red cups, paper plates, and phat bags of weed. So why should this year be any different? Anticipating your loan for this year, you decided to skip saving for school costs and pay for the good stuff first—like that new video game console you wanted, the cruise to Mexico with your boys for Spring Break, and a whole lot of beer and expensive booze. Then you get this year's financial aid package and realize you're not getting as much as last time. You're all out of cash and you haven't even paid tuition yet . . . WTF?

The WTF Approach to Paying Out of F*#!-ing Pocket

➤ **OPTION #1:** *Get a Job Fast*

Believe it or not, it's relatively easy to get a job in a college town. Unless, of course, you are going to school in California, Arizona, New Mexico, or Texas, where illegal aliens will work far harder and for far less than you.

➤ **OPTION #2:** *Sell Yourself*

That's right, head over to your local sperm bank and make a deposit. You can make several deposits in a week and get paid in cash. You might as well get paid to do something you do for free four to five times a day!

➤ **OPTION #3:** *Sell Your Blood*

You won't be able to make as many deposits as with the sperm, but it still pays. Don't mix this with Option #2 though. That can give you AIDS.

➤ **OPTION #4:** *Hock Your Roommate's Shit*

He probably has something of value. Take it, sell it, and then stage a break in. You can report it to the police and file a claim.

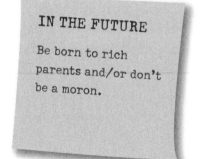

for the ladies . . .
Become a prostitute, duh!

IN THE FUTURE

Be born to rich parents and/or don't be a moron.

Chapter 2

Dorm Life

13. An Epidemic of Crabs Breaks Out in Your Dorm

Lately you've been dancing around like a jerk. At first you thought it was the new laundry detergent you were using, then you thought it was some kind of food allergy, but now you're not the only one doing the shuffle. Other students in the dorms seem a little extra fidgety as of late. The good news: It's not epilepsy. The bad news: You've got crabs—and so does half your dorm! Here's what to do when your genitals have been turned into a twenty-four-hour seafood buffet . . .

The WTF Approach to Recovering from F*#!-ing Crabs

➤ STEP #1: *Get Treatment*

Remember those lice outbreaks in grade school? Same treatment, different patch of hair. You can pick up a lice kit in any drug store. After application of the pesticide, you must then comb out your uninvited guests. It is important to treat the infected area thoroughly, which will include anal hairs and those on the thigh area. It is also a good idea to treat anyone whom you're in a sexual relationship with to reduce the chance of reinfestation. You might want to make a night of it: little bottle of wine, little crab removal . . . hot!

➤ STEP #2: *Damage Control*

Now that you're clean—of crabs anyway—it's time to clean house. Although the primary way to contract crabs is from sexual contact, it's also possible to get them from infected bedding, towels, and clothes. Wash everything thoroughly in hot water to kill the creepy crawlies.

➤ STEP # 3: *Shave It Baby!*

That's right, shave it all off. It may sound extreme, but this way you won't have to use the ointments or a comb. Start from scratch. Strippers and porn stars do it. Why can't you? And for you crabby guys out there, shaving your pubes might make your dick look bigger. Bonus!

WTFACT: Studies show that crabs reproduce faster than Mormons—though they are far less annoying.

To Blame or Not to Blame?

There's plenty of sexual revelry in your dorm, and not everyone is as clean as you. However, don't waste your time trying to figure out who to blame for this outbreak. Crabs spread fast on bodies and clothing. You can even get crabs from a toilet seat (don't bother squatting—crabs can jump). So unless you plan on never taking a dump in public again, you need to accept that crabs are an occupational hazard of college life.

WTF: UP CLOSE AND PERSONAL

The Great Crab Outbreak of 1993

Hurricanes are bad, earthquakes are worse, and tornadoes are just plain scary, but until you live through a crab outbreak you don't know the true nature of terror.

It was a chilly night in 1993 when the crabs took control of my dorm at East Strousburg University. I'll never forget the sight of hundreds of girls running down the halls scratching themselves wildly, as if they were possessed by demons. Horrible. Just horrible.

The outbreak was so bad that we all had to leave the dorm for the weekend so that it could be decontaminated before we returned. Rumor has it that regular decontamination efforts didn't work, and the school had to hire a priest to finally oust the little bastards. Luckily, with God on his side, he was successful, and we could return that Monday to a crab-free environment for the rest of the semester.

But it wasn't over for me. I still can't bring myself to eat shellfish to this day. At least, not intentionally.

—JM

IN THE FUTURE . . .

Examine your partner's genitals closely before engaging in sexual conduct. Before doing the deed, head down south and look carefully at the pubes, if you see something move, abort! If not, just pump and pray.

14. You Clog the Only Stall on Your Floor

You're not actually sure what the hell you ate last night, but whatever it was, it didn't agree with you. You just spent a good forty-five minutes in the dorm bathroom clearing the pipes, so to speak. Done, you take a moment to look at your accomplishment. Damn, how the hell did that even fit inside you? Not your problem anymore, it's out and all you need to do is flush and get on with your day . . . but not so fast. You push down on the toilet's lever only to find the waste isn't going down but coming up, and up, and up. *Shit!* Literally.

The WTF Approach to Dealing with a Clogged F*#!-ing Toilet

➤ OPTION #1: *Take Off*

Get the hell out of there and let someone else take the blame. You're feeling light on your feet now anyhow, so you should be able to get away quickly.

➤ OPTION #2: *Close the Lid and Pray*

Shut the bowl tight and hope the mountain of feces doesn't escape. Put a sign on the door that says out of order—or full of shit—either will work.

➤ OPTION #3: *Trash the Bathroom*

Make it look like some drunken students ransacked the can in the middle of the night. Then report it. You will look like the good guy in this scenario.

➤ OPTION #4: *Mark Your Territory*

Take the shit out and smear it on the wall and claim that stall is yours. No one else will go near it—or you—ever again.

WTFACT: The human small intestine can reach up to eight meters in length. Why do you want to know that? Because all knowledge is important, fuck-face.

IN THE FUTURE . . .

Get a monthly enema—if you can't afford one, have one of your buddies shove a hose up your ass and turn the water pressure on high.

WHATEVER THE F*#! YOU DO— DON'T FLUSH THESE:

- Cotton balls
- Unused herpes ointment
- Condoms
- Chopped up body parts
- Newborns

15. You Catch Your Roommate Cross-Dressing

Living with someone else can be tough. It's not easy to adjust to another person's habits and share a common space. But at least you prepared yourself for that change. What you weren't prepared for was walking into your dorm and finding your roommate in a tube top and mini-skirt. That's right, your roommate likes to wear women's clothing. And what's worse, he has really bad taste.

The WTF Approach to Living with a Dude in a F*#!-ing Skirt

➤ STEP #1: *Deal with It*

So he likes to dress up like a chick? So does Eddie Izzard, and he's famous. As long as he is not bothering you, let him do what makes him happy—unless he wears white after Labor Day . . . completely unacceptable.

➤ STEP #2: *Rent* Sex and the City *on DVD*

If he's going to dress like a chick, he might as well get a better sense of style. Have him watch a few episodes as a guide. Careful though, you don't want to make him too hot. It would suck if you came home drunk and tried to hook up with him thinking he was actually a girl . . .

➤ STEP #3: *When in Rome . . .*

If you can't beat him, join him. Some women's clothing can be very liberating. Hey, it could be fun. You guys can be the new *Bosom Buddies*.

Be Careful What You Wish For

If this little fetish of his really bothers you, ask to be moved into another room. But be warned, you could end up with a roommate who wears the same guys clothing every single day without doing laundry. What's worse: a dude in women's lingerie or month-old underwear?

***WTF*ACT:** Most cross-dressers are heterosexual men, while most transsexuals are homosexual men. If you want to know the difference, look it up jackass. Aren't you in college for crying out loud?

FAMOUS MEN WHO CROSS-DRESSED IN REAL LIFE:

- Eddie Izzard
- J. Edgar Hoover
- Milton Berle
- Divine

FAMOUS MEN WHO CROSS-DRESSED IN THE MOVIES:

- Dustin Hoffman in *Tootsie*
- The Wayans Brothers in *White Chicks*
- Martin Lawrence in *Big Mama's House*
- Bea Arthur in *everything*

IN THE FUTURE . . .

Do a little research on the guy you are planning on living with. If you find out that he played Juliet in his high school production of *Romeo and Juliet*, request another roommate immediately.

16. You Go to Do Laundry, but All the Machines Are Taken

You've put it off as long as you could. You've gone through every shirt and pair of pants in your wardrobe, and now your clothes are so dirty they are practically walking around by themselves. And to top that off, you have a hot date tonight. You really, *really* need to do laundry, but as usual, all the machines are taken.

The WTF Approach to Cleaning Your F*#!-ing Clothes

►OPTION #1: *Double Up*

Toss your stuff in with someone else's. Make sure to stand guard. You will need to retrieve all of your things before that person comes back.

►OPTION #2: *Use an Occupied Machine*

Desperate times call for desperate measures. This is tricky, though, and must be carefully executed:

1. Remove the clothes out of one machine and place on the counter.
2. Take the clothes from another machine that's just been started and place them in the machine you initially emptied.
3. Put your stuff in the machine you emptied last.

This way when the guy with the clothes in the first machine comes back and sees his stuff wet on the counter, he will find someone else's in his machine—and blame him. You will still need to stand guard though in case the guy from the second machine comes back first.

➤ OPTION #3: *Use the Sink*

Only wash what you will be wearing that night. And make sure you have a couple hours to let the clothes air-dry. Be certain the clothes are clean before hanging them out to dry.

NOTE: Toothpaste does *not* make a good laundry detergent.

➤ OPTION #4: *Wear Your Roommate's Clothes*

Just make sure not to ruin them. If so, make sure to read "You Ruin Your Roommate's Brand-New Jacket after Wearing It . . . Without Asking" (page 47).

➤ OPTION #5: *Head to Another Dorm*

Suck it up and take your dirty shit to another dorm. Don't go to the girls' dorm—those machines are *always* taken.

➤ OPTION #6: *Fuck It*

Just wear the least dirty thing you have, then take your date to a crowded, sweaty, smoke-filled frat party. All the repugnant odors, including yours, will blend in.

IN THE FUTURE . . .

Always save a clean outfit for such an occasion. You don't have to do much in college to get laid, but at the very least make sure you're not a smelly piece of shit.

17. You're Trying to Sleep and Your Roommate Is Having Sex

Now, screwing in front of roommates is par for the course in college, but sometimes a person's got to get some sleep. Lately, it seems like every night you wake up to what you think is a sex dream—a very vivid and loud sex dream—only to realize it ain't no dream—it's a nightmare! A real, live nightmare. You open your eyes yet again to find your roommate's skinny white ass high in the sky pounding away at a very vocal, boozed-up floozy.

The WTF Approach to Battling Your Roommate's F*#!-ing Booty Call

➤ OPTION #1: *Leave*

Just quietly slip out and go crash on the couch in the common area. Its sucks, but one day you will be able to repay the favor to your roommate.

➤ OPTION #2: *Go Off*

That's right, turn on the lights and start screaming. This will surely stop the lovebirds in their tracks and send her out the door. Your roommate will probably kick your ass, but at least when he's done you can get some shut-eye.

► **OPTION #3:** *Get It on Tape*

Since you're not sleeping, you might as well do something to pass the time. After they're done, post it on YouTube. Chances are your roommate will never see that girl again and he'll probably have a hard time getting any other chick to go home with him.

► **OPTION #4:** *Drown It Out*

Put on your iPod and turn up the volume. Listen to the sounds of spring and pretend you are in a peaceful green meadow far, far away from your roommate's gyrating.

► **OPTION #5:** *Join In*

Shit, the girl might be into it. Just walk up and see if you can stick yourself in her mouth. If your roommate objects, stick yourself in his mouth to shut him up.

IN THE FUTURE . . .

If you and your roommate plan on getting some ass on a regular basis, you should institute a code system using different color clothes. Place an item of clothing that's the necessary color on the doorknob outside the door. See the chart below.

COLOR	MEANING
White	Come back in an hour.
Blue	Come back in two hours.
Red	Come back tomorrow.
Black	Go get help.
Yellow	Join in.

18. You Didn't Know a Webcam Was On in Your Room

The stares. The whispers. The giggles. Every time you leave your room it's like you're walking around with a sign on your back—and you have no idea why. Then one day you come across a video on YouTube. Hey, that looks like your college. Hey, that even looks like your dorm room. Hey, that even looks like . . . WTF? Is that *you*? And is that *live*? Your roommate hid a webcam somewhere in your room, and you have unknowingly been starring in your own real-life *Truman Show*. Not to worry, what have you been doing in your room besides sleeping, playing video games, eating . . . oh no, jerking off! No wondering people are staring at you. You're a celebrity.

The WTF Approach to Handling Your Fifteen F*#!-ing Minutes

➤ **STEP #1:** *Work It*

Now that you know you're being taped, make this one show worth watching. Lose weight, learn to dance, or grow a bigger dick. Might not hurt to actually score a chick once in a while too.

➤ STEP #2: *Sue Him*

This is a serious violation of privacy, and you could get a nice lawsuit settlement. However, if your roommate is broke and not worth suing, skip down to Step #3.

➤ STEP #3: *Kill Him*

Turn the webcam off first so no one can prove it. Now that's a great ending to your reality show!

> **NOTE:** It's an urban legend that if your roommate dies during the school year you'll get an automatic 4.0, and a lot of sympathy sex.

WTF *Reality Show Ideas*

We here at *WTF* pitched a few reality show ideas to producers in Hollywood. So far we haven't heard back . . .

Joe Millionaire with No Arms or Legs

This one ups the ante on the successful reality show *Joe Millionaire* (in which an average Joe is introduced to a horde of hot chicks as a multimillionaire) when it's revealed that this average Joe not only has no money, but he has no arms or legs either. Imagine the look on the chosen girl's face when he takes off all four plastic prostheses . . . hysterical!

Joe Millionaire with a Brain Tumor

We're laughing already. Can you imagine the tears when the chosen girl finds out her soul mate has less than six months to live! LOL!

Joe Millionaire: Convicted Murderer

A cold-blooded killer! She didn't see that one coming! Ha, ha, ha!

19. You Get Caught with a Girl in Your Room After Hours

First off, congratulations are in order. You're doing what you should be doing in college: screwing around. So pat yourself on the back (even if she was a beast). Now, as for getting caught with her in your room after hours, well, those are the breaks of a strict cohabitation policy. Here are some ways to deal with this situation before you're thrown out of the building.

The WTF Approach to Beating F*#!-ing Bullshit Rules

➤ OPTION #1: *Stop Having Sex*

You should not be having sex before you are married anyway. Don't you know that is a sin, you little piece of shit? What would Jesus say? We mean, if he didn't hang out with hookers like Mary Magdalene, that is.

► OPTION #2: *Bang Elsewhere*

When it comes to finding a way to have sex, human beings (especially dudes) reach new heights of creativity. You may not be able to write a sonnet, compose a symphony, or even take a decent photograph, but you will sure as hell find *somewhere* to screw—no matter what it takes.

► OPTION # 3: *Keep Doing It in Your Room*

What are the chances they'll catch you twice? Keep breaking the rules; after all, that's what college is for. If you do end up getting the boot, at least everyone in the dorm will know why. Come on, you couldn't ask for better press than that.

THE 5 BEST PLACES TO HAVE SEX:

1. Ferris wheel
2. Gondola in Venice
3. Taco Bell bathroom (speaking from experience here)
4. Jail (WTF else is there to do?)
5. In the air during a skydive

THE 5 WORST PLACES TO HAVE SEX:

1. A tight rope
2. In Los Angeles during a riot
3. An internment camp
4. Siberia (it just seems like it must suck there)
5. Dante's seventh circle of hell

20. You Get Caught with Beer in Your Room

You and your friends are right in the middle of some serious gaming while downing a couple of beers. What a great day, until your RA pops in unexpectedly and finds the beer. There is a no alcohol policy on campus and, guess what, you just got nabbed.

The WTF Approach to Avoiding a F*#!-ing Write-Up

➤ OPTION 1#: *Drink Up*

Down it, bitch! Your RA can't prove you're drinking if there isn't any alcohol. If he smells the alcohol, tell him it's not beer, but that you are drinking your own piss according to this new cleansing diet you heard about.

➤ OPTION #2: *Make It a Party*

Get your RA wasted and let him join in. Most RAs are a bunch of nerds that are in desperate need of fun. Show them what you're actually supposed to do in school.

➤ OPTION #3: *Beg for Mercy*

Get down on your knees and beg the prick to overlook it. RAs are like cops and other assholes—they just like the power.

PROFESSOR TIP: Most campuses have a no-alcohol policy. But that doesn't mean you shouldn't keep alcohol in your room, you just need to be clever about it. Hide vodka in a water bottle or keep beer in the ceiling panels.

IN THE FUTURE . . .

Do drugs that you can hide easily. Pills are a good bet. Enjoy!

21. Your Roommate Eats All Your Food

College is a great learning experience. You not only improve your academic skills, you also learn to live with people—and that some people are not worth living with.

The WTF Approach to Stopping Your F*#!-ing All-Consuming Roomie

➤ STEP #1: *Label It*

The time for sharing is over. Put labels on everything you buy and tell your thieving roommate to do the same. That'll put an end to that "was that yours?" game.

➤ STEP # 2: *Poison Your Food*

If the labels don't stop him, this'll show him. Buy something you know he likes and lace it with something that will *at least* make him sick, if not kill him. Be careful,

if you do murder him, not to get caught—you don't get to pick your roommates in jail either.

WTF: UP CLOSE AND PERSONAL

Back before I was the internationally renowned author of the *WTF*? series, I rented a room the size of a latrine (and almost as smelly) in Staten Island, New York, for $400 a month.

My landlord and roommate was Manuel—a five-foot-tall,

handicapped Mexican who, rumor had it, was dying of AIDS. Manuel dressed in a kimono and sported a half-mustache. (Yes, he would only shave half of his mustache.) And despite his dark skin, jet-black hair, and the fact he was born and raised in Mexico City, Manuel claimed he was Scandinavian. As a tribute to his heritage, Manuel decorated his room with posters, paintings, and statues of famous Nordic gods and heroes.

A nineteen-year-old community college student at the time, I was always broke and chose to spend what I had on beer rather than food. So what did I do? I ate Manuel's, mostly his mozzarella cheese. You see, if you take a little slice at a time, there's a good chance the person won't notice. However, Manuel did. He would yell at me in his thick Mexican accent: "Stop eating my cheese!

You are making my Viking blood boil!" (I am not making this up.)

Luckily, however, Manuel had a crush on me (what, the kimono didn't tip you off?), so he let me get away with my cheese-eating activities. Oh, college.

—GB

IN THE FUTURE . . .

Find a roommate with an eating disorder—specifically anorexia. You don't want a bulimic vomiting all over the joint. You can also ask to be roomed with a vegan. They don't eat anything. Plus, they always have weed.

22. You Ruin Your Roommate's Brand-New Jacket after Wearing It . . . Without Asking

You should have asked. Sure, yes, of course. But you knew he wouldn't let you borrow it, and you just *had* to wear it. You really wanted to impress that girl, and it looks better on you anyhow. That said, he's going to kill you when he realizes that his new black jacket is covered in polka dots—courtesy of your semen.

The WTF Approach to Covering Your F*#!-ing Tracks

▶ OPTION #1: *Fake a Burglary*

Throw everything on the floor, empty the drawers, and knock everything off the shelves. Then make sure to call the campus police and file a report. Call your roommate in hysterics so it's more believable. Make sure to throw his jacket away—it's more likely that the burglars stole it than dowsed it in sperm. Also, take this opportunity to steal some of his stuff and sell it.

▶ OPTION #2: *Set the Room on Fire*

This will be fun, but you'll lose all your shit too. Then again, if you had shit to begin with, you wouldn't keep mooching off him.

➤ OPTION #3: *Buy a New One*

If you aren't an asshole, then confess and buy him a new jacket.

➤ OPTION #4: *Tell a Good Story*

If you spilled some jizz on the jacket because your date was blowing you under the table at the restaurant, then he might forgive you—especially if you give him her number. Remember, guys love stories, and a good blowjob story always trumps a ruined jacket. After all, guys only buy good clothes to get blowjobs.

➤ OPTION # 5: *Drug Him*

Drug him up and put the jacket on him, then unzip his pants. He'll wake up, blame himself, and you'll be off the hook.

WHAT THE F*#! IS UP WITH . . .
BORROWING

There is too much borrowing in this society, especially in college. Can I borrow a pen? Can I borrow a piece of paper? Can I borrow your bong? It's too much. And not to mention borrowing, like sharing, is a form of socialism, and socialism is the devil. Didn't you learn that? Of course not, damn liberal elitist professors!

IN THE FUTURE . . .

Tell him to go to hell. So you took his jacket and ruined it? You can take him. Be a man. WTF?

for the ladies . . .

Girls are more skeptical and less forgiving. You might have to shoot her.

23. Your Roommate Is Gay and After Your Ass

When you met him, you figured he was just a trendy and fashionable guy. While you wouldn't be caught dead in a tight, hot-pink shirt, this was the University of California—and he was a local. But then other things made you raise an eyebrow, like his four different moisturizers, his Rogers and Hammerstein DVD collection, and his favorite bedtime T-shirt that just reads *Slut*. But so what? You're in college now. It's time to be more open-minded, right? But then things get uncomfortable, like when he says that "you're hot." One night he asks if you would like to sleep under his tented blanket. Yikes!

The WTF Approach to Dealing with F*#!-ing Unrequited Love

➤ **OPTION #1:** *Request to Be Moved*

You are not the only one looking to ditch your rooming situation. Like marriages, most dorm relationships don't last.

➤ **OPTION #2:** *File a Sexual Harassment Suit*

Go to the Dean of Students and explain your story. If your gay roommate goes too far, you could have a case. Claim something outrageous, like say he asked you if you put a public hair on the top of his beer can. This may not have worked for Anita Hill, but then again, you're not a black female.

WTFACT: Anita Hill famously accused Supreme Court Justice Clarence Thomas of sexual harassment during his confirmation hearings. She alleged, among other things, that Judge Thomas had asked her if she put a pubic hair in his coke. Yummy.

➤ OPTION #3: *No Means No!*

If you're the violent type, welcome his unwanted advance with a punch in the nose or, in the case of the tent scenario, his erection. Be prepared to face legal consequences for this terrible act. Also, most gays keep in pretty good shape, so chances are he'll end up beating the shit out of *you.*

NOTE: We here at *WTF* do not condone violence in any way—and are definitely not liable for any such acts. Your stupidity is your problem.

YOUR ROOMMATE MAY BE IN LOVE WITH YOU IF . . .

❏ He's ever made a mixed CD for you.
❏ He has a suspiciously large number of pictures of you two on his MySpace page.
❏ There's an indent on the edge of your bed where he sits at night to watch you sleep.
❏ The milkshakes he brings you sometimes taste *way* too salty.

What If You Are In Love with Your Roommate?

Your roommate thinks you guys are best friends. You talk about girls, school, and just about everything. But what you don't talk about is your growing desire to bang him. Here's a quick rundown on what to do . . .

1. Sabotage his relationships. If you can't have him, then why should anyone else?

2. Bang the same girl together. You'll at least get to have sex with him, if not actually *with* him.
3. Confess. Just lay your cards (and dick) on the table. After the awkwardness of the above, he's probably figured it out anyway.

COLLEGE KID QUOTE

"I caught my roommate masturbating in my bed. And I was like, 'Dude what the fuck are you doing, bro? That's my bed.' And he was like, 'Oh, I'm sorry.' And then I saw that he was wearing my underwear. And I was like, 'Dude, that's my fucking underwear.' And he was all, 'Oh, I'm sorry.' And then I saw that he had a photo of me next to him, and I was like totally freaked out and yelled, '*Dude*, that's my photo! What are you gay or something?' And he goes, 'No!' And I'm like, 'Yes, you are!' And he's like, 'Okay. Yes, I am. I'm sorry.' And I was just like, 'Wow, gross.' And then I walked out or whatever."

—Danny, freshman at University of Colorado

24. Your Loser Roommate Is Getting More Action Than You

You don't like to be a spoilsport, but this is getting ridiculous. Every time you come home with your head down after striking out yet again, you open the door to see your roommate with his head between another chick's legs.

The WTF Approach to Getting More F*#!-ing Ass

➤ **OPTION #1: *Watch and Learn***

If you have a good view of your friend while he's banging away, pay attention and take some notes. Maybe he's getting laid more than you for a reason—he's better at it.

➤ **OPTION #2: *Get Sloppy Seconds***

If he is such a hot shot, maybe he can help you out by convincing the chicks he brings over to screw you after he is done with them. Better to have sloppy seconds

than to cry every night with your hand down your pants wishing that you were dead.

➤ **OPTION #3: *Get Plastic Surgery***

Maybe you can't get laid as much as your roommate because you're a fat ugly pig. If you're chubby, get liposuction. If you're ugly, get a face-lift and a nose job. And if you have a little pecker, get a penile implant—or just go after Asian chicks.

➤ OPTION #4: *Sabotage Him*

Ruin his relationships by leaving other girls' numbers in his pants, or put bras and panties and other dumb shit like that in his bed. If you aren't getting laid, might as well spoil it for him. You can also play the good guy and tell his girlfriends that he's a prick and cheats on them. Maybe they'll do you just to get back at him.

➤ OPTION #5: *Cut His Dick Off*

Pull a Lorena Bobbit and chop his pecker clean off. Then take a good look at it and see what a real man's dick is supposed to look like.

WTFACT: Your roommate is better than you. Loser!

POP QUIZ

If two college roommates are both at a party and hitting on the same girl and one of the guys grabs her boob and the other guy grabs her ass, at what speed will their balls be kicked?

A. 100 mph
B. 50 mph
C. It will hurt no matter what.

Answer: C

IN THE FUTURE . . .

Make sure your roommate is lamer than you. If your roommate looks too cool when you meet him, request another roommate right away. Don't overestimate yourself and think you'll turn as cool as him.

25. You Accidentally Burn Down Your Dorm

Every student heads off to college with the basic necessities. Clothes, school supplies, and a hot plate. Can't live without that hot plate. From making soup to making meth, it's a must-have. The only problem is sometimes you forget to turn that shit off when you're done. One day on your way back to the dorms, you notice several fire trucks and hundreds of students outside. Looks like some asshole left his hot plate on and burned down the dorm. Oh wait, that asshole was you. Bummer.

The WTF Approach to Handling F*#!-ing Accidental Arson

➤ OPTION #1: *Take Off*

Just split and never return. Fuck it.

➤ OPTION #2: *Break Out the Marshmallows*

Shit, you can't do anything about it now, so might as well make the most of it. Material things don't matter anyhow. Make s'mores for everyone and maybe they'll forgive you.

➤ OPTION #3: *Sue*

That's right: sue. Sue the company that makes the hot plate. Even if this model wasn't defective, their hot plates should have an automatic turn-off switch. They should know only drunk, stupid, and high college students use these. Settle out of court and drop out of school. You'll be rich; you don't need a degree now.

➤ OPTION #4: *Become an Arsonist*

Fire is pretty. Get some more hot plates or, better yet, some matches and gasoline and burn down all kinds of shit. Come up with a cool arsonist name like "Franky the Fire Starter" and become infamous.

NOTE: Congratulations on your new career choice. Way to prove to your parents that you don't need a college degree for *everything*. Just don't come crying to us when you can't beat your arson rap, or give yourself third-degree burns over 90 percent of your body.

THINGS THAT WILL SET ON FIRE:

- Alcohol
- Aerosol hairspray
- Bedding
- Gasoline
- Dirty underwear

THINGS THAT ARE FUN TO SET ON FIRE:

- Fireworks
- Homework
- Ex-girlfriends
- Feces
- Malibu

WTF: UP CLOSE AND PERSONAL

I once burned down a hotel room in a small town in northern Laos. Let me explain . . .

After college, I backpacked throughout Southeast Asia for a few months. One night, during a binge, I apparently left a candle burning in my room when I went out. The candle somehow started my backpack on fire, which contained my toiletries—including an aerosol deodorant can. The bag blew like a stick of dynamite, scattering scorched pieces throughout the room and ceiling.

One of my travel companions came to find me at a bar to tell of the inferno. In his thick Norwegian accent, he said, "Your voom Greig is on fire!" I laughed and shrugged, thinking he was bullshitting. However, I returned to the hotel to find the owner and his family cleaning up my disaster of a room. Luckily, my money and passport were hidden behind the mirror in the bathroom, which the fire did not reach.

When the hotel owner told me that we would "work this out in the morning," I tried to escape into the night, but the town was so small there was no late-night transportation. I was stuck. So I went with Plan B: Tell them that my money was in my bag and that because it was destroyed, I was left with nothing. Yes, that would be my story.

In the end, they took me to jail as a negotiation ploy when I refused to pay the full $400 damage cost. On the way to the station, I worked out a deal to pay about $130. Overall, I am very proud of my negotiating skills that day—though it might have been better not to have burned down the room in the first place.

—GB

26. Your Roommate Is Masturbating Every Time You Go to Your Room

We've all heard the urban legend that if you masturbate too much you'll go blind. This was started by mothers who couldn't stand the sight of their little boys treating their privates like an amusement park. But if this old wives' tale is true, your new roommate would not only have gone blind, he would have lost his sense of hearing, taste, and smell. Now, you have always been a big supporter of taking care of business, but the last time you counted, your roommate was jerking off at least twenty times a day. Defiled tube socks are scattered all over the room—like Christmas stockings at porn star Peter North's house. *Enough.*

The WTF Approach to Stopping the F*#!-ing Whack Fest

➤ STEP #1: *Talk to Him*

Sit him down and tell him that if he keeps it up, he will run out of sperm and never be able to reproduce. While that might be a good thing for the world, it should scare him into moderation.

➤ STEP #2: *Find Him a Girl*

If your little talk didn't work, search high and low to find him a girl to help him work off all that pent-up tension. Just make sure she loves sex as much as him. At least, if he still whacks off this much with a girlfriend, it'll be her problem now.

➤ STEP #3: *Tape Him Doing It*

Talking didn't work. Sex didn't work. Now it's time for embarrassment. Set up a webcam to plaster his pleasuring all across the Internet. Once everyone knows about his extracurricular activities, he'll be so embarrassed he might stop masturbating altogether.

THE CIRCLE JERKS

You could always put on some porn, make some popcorn, and make a night of it. Invite all your friends over and have a circle jerk. Whoever comes last, cleans up—with their face. Who knows? You might substitute this new fun activity for Tuesday night poker.

➤ STEP #4: *Cut Off His Dick*

He can't touch what isn't there. Drug him, cut his dick off, and then drop him off at the hospital. The doctors should be able to reattach it, but he will think twice about tugging on it after that.

SLANG TERMS FOR MASTURBATING:

Answer the bone-a-phone

Assault on a friendly weapon

Backstroke roulette

Baiting your hook

Batting practice

Beating the bishop

Beating your meat

Being your own best friend

Blow your load

Bludgeon the beefsteak

Boppin' your bologna

Box the Jesuit (16th–17th century!)

Buffing the banana

Burping the worm

Butter your corn

Calling down for more mayo

Calling all cum

Carrying weight

Changing your oil

Charm the cobra

Choke the sheriff and wait for the posse to come

Choke your chicken

Clean the pipes

Clean your rifle

Clubbing Eddy

Couch hockey for one

Crank the shank

Crown the king

Custer's last stand

Date Miss Michigan

Date Mother Palm and her five daughters

Devil's handshake (Catholic school)

Diddle

Dishonorable discharge

Disseminating

Doddle whacking

Doodle your noodle

Do the dew

Drain the vein

Dropping a line

Dropping stomach pancakes

Fist your mister

Five against one

Five-finger knuckle shuffle

Flute solo

Freeing the Willies

Frigging the love muscle (British)

Getting in touch with your manhood

Getting in touch with yourself

Getting to know yourself personally in the "biblical sense"

Giving it a tug

Greasing your bone

Hack the hog

Hands-on training

Hand to gland combat

Having a Roy
(Australian)

Have one off the wrist

Hitchhike under the
big top

Holding all the cards

Holding your sausage
hostage

Hone your bone

Hump your fist

Hump your hose

Humpin' air

Ironing some wrinkles

Jack hammer

Jack off

Jackin' the beanstalk

J Arthur Rank (British
rhyming slang—wank)

Jelly roll

Jenny Macarthy jaunt

Jerk off

Jerkin' the gherkin

Jiggle the jewelry

Jimmying your Joey

Knuckle shuffle on your
piss pump

Launching the hand
shuttle

Making nut butter

Making yogurt

Mangle the midget

Manipulate the mango

Manual override

Masonic secret
self-handshake

Massage your muscle

Massage your purple-
headed warrior

Measuring for condoms

Meeting with Palmala
Handerson

Milking the lizard

Milkywaying

Molding hot plastic

Nerk your throbber

Oil the glove

One-handed clapping

One-man show

One-man tug-o-war

Paddle the pickle

Pam Anderson polka

Pat the Robertson

Peel some chilis

Playing with Dick

Playing with Susi Palmer
and her five friends

Play pocket pool

Play the organ

Play the pisser

Play the piss pipe

Play the skin flute

Play the stand-up organ

Playing with the snake

Playing your instrument

Plunk your twanger

Pocket pinball

Pocket pool

Polish the chrome dome

Polish the rocket

Polish the sword

Pounding your pud

Pudwhacking

Pud wrestling

Puddin'

Pull the root

Pulling the wire

Pulling your goalie

Pull your taffy

Pumping for pleasure

Pump the python

Punchin' the clown

Punchin' the munchkin

Punishing Percy

Punishing the bishop

Ride the great white knuckler

Rolling the fleshy blunt

Roman helmet rumba

Ropin' the longhorn

Roughing up the suspect

Rounding up the tadpoles

Runka (Swedish)

Scratching the itch

Seasonin' your meat

Sending out the troops

Shaking hands with Abe Lincoln

Shaking hands with the governor

Shaking hands with shorty

Shake the snake

Shifting gears

Shooting Sherman

Shucking Bubba

Slammin' the salami

Slappin' Pappy

Slapping the clown

Slap boxing the one-eyed champ

Slap my happy sacks

Slapping the cyclops

Slinging jelly

Sloppy Joe's last stand

Sloppy sign language

Stroke the stallion

Smacking your sister

Spank your monkey

Spear chucking

Spreading the mayo

Spunk the monk

Squeeze the cream from the flesh Twinkie

Squeeze the lemon

Squeezing the tube of toothpaste

Squeezing the burrito

Staff meeting

Stall clapping

Stroke off

Stroking it

Stroking your goat

Stroke your poker

Taking a shake break

Tame the wild hog

Tap the turkey

Tease the python

Tease the weasle

Tenderize the meat

The erky jerk

The sticky page Rumba

Threading a needle

Throw off a batch

Throwin' down

Thump the pump

Tickle the Elmo

Tickle the pickle

Toss off

Toss the boss

Toss the turkey

Tugging your tapioca tube

Tugging your tubesnake

Tug of war with cyclops

Tuning the antenna

Turning Japanese (UK—one step beyond wanking)

Tussle with your muscle

Unwrapping the pepperoni

Varnishing the cane

Wailing

Walk the dog

Walking Willie the one-eyed wonder worm

Wank (British)

Waxing the dolphin

Wax your Jackson

Whipping the one-eyed wonder weasle

Whipping the pony

Whipping the window washer

White-water wristing

Whizzin' jizzim

Wiggling your worm

Winding the Jack-in-the-box

Wonk your conker

Working a cramp out of your muscle

Working your Willy

Wrestling the eel

Wring out your rope

Wring your thing

Yahtzee

Yank my doodle (it's a dandy)

Yank off

Yank the yodle

Yank your crank

for the ladies . . .

Auditioning the finger puppets

Beating around the bush

Clam bake for one

Dialing the rotary phone

Engaging in safe sex

Get to know yourself

Get a stinky pinky

Hitchhiking south

Muffin buffin'

Paddling the pink canoe

Polishing the pearl

Tiptoe through the twolips

Washing your fingers

Chapter 3

Classin' It Up

27. You Come from a Family of Doctors . . . But You Can't Stand the Sight of Blood

Ever since you were a kid you knew your destiny: You would be a doctor. Just like your dad and his dad before him. You started off well. You made your dad proud when you were accepted to his alma mater, and even prouder when you got into the exclusive pre-med program. It seemed as though nothing could stop you from being all that you were expected to be. And then you realized something kind of important: You can't stand the sight of blood.

The WTF Approach to Battling F*#!-ing Hemaphobia

➤ OPTION #1: *Be a Podiatrist*

If you can find a way of getting through medical school without being a little bitch, you'll never have to see blood again if you choose the foot doctor route. Sure, it's not exactly the surgeon that your dad wanted you to be, but you will technically be a doctor. Better yet—be a gynecologist. (Just don't see patients during that time of the month.)

➤ OPTION #2: *Be a Chiropractor*

Sometimes people mistake these crooks for doctors, even though they never went to med school. You get to wear a white coat, overcharge patients, and grow a beard just like a doctor. The only difference: you don't actually perform any real service. Win-win.

➤ OPTION #3: *Get a Doctorate in Drama*

They never specifically said what *kind* of doctor, so just act as though you misunderstood. You should be able to pull it off, seeing as how you studied so much drama. And who knows, you might book a gig on television as a doctor. House seems to know what he's talking about.

➤ OPTION #4: *Play Doctor*

It's more fun anyhow. You don't need to be a doctor to get a woman to take her clothes off and let you examine her. But it does help.

YOU MIGHT BE A BAD DOCTOR IF . . .

- ❑ You went to med school in the Caribbean.
- ❑ You think the heart is shaped like a Valentine.
- ❑ You always lose at the game Operation. Damn funny bone.
- ❑ Your patients usually end up in the morgue—and you're a chiropodist.
- ❑ You're a gentile.

IN THE FUTURE . . .

Tell Dad and Granddad to screw. So what if your family wants you to be a doctor? Be a man and choose your own path. Go into porn and call yourself Dr. Fuck, or become a rapper like Dr. Dre.

28. Your Parents Are Up Your Ass Because Your Major Is Undeclared

>>>>> *What's your major?* It's perhaps the most commonly asked question in college behind the omnipresent: *What dorm do you live in? Where is the keg?* and *Do you have a condom?* And yet, despite mounting pressure from your peers and parents to choose a major, you just can't seem to make up your mind.

The WTF Approach to Choosing a F*#!-ing Major

➤ STEP #1: *Examine Your Interests*

Besides *Family Guy* and porn, what do you like to do? If you can't come up with an answer in a few minutes, you should probably watch a little *Family Guy* and then whack off to some porn. It might help clear your head so you can think straight.

➤ STEP #2: *Examine Your Abilities*

If you can't do basic arithmetic then you should probably steer clear of accounting. Then again, if you can't do basic arithmetic, you should probably steer clear of life and commit suicide for being a moron.

➤ STEP #3: *Examine Your Dick*

No reason in particular, we just figured since you were examining things and had nothing else to do right now it might pass the time.

➤ STEP #4: *Take Classes*

Don't worry about your major right now, and just take classes that engage you. Think of this time as a kind of courtship period between you and your intellect before you commit her to a specific discipline. In other words, bang the shit out of every subject that interests you before you choose one to marry.

➤ STEP #5: *Major in Communications*

Trust us; it's a total fucking joke.

WTFACT: According to recent studies, one in four people have claimed psychology as their major at one time during their college tenure. But just because you majored in psychology for a half a semester doesn't give you the right to psychoanalyze that hot girl who won't hook up with you. Yeah we get it—she has daddy issues. Who doesn't?

How to Choose a Major

Before you pick a major, you need to be able to recognize which majors pertain to which professions.

POP QUIZ

Match the following majors with their corresponding professions.

1. Math
2. English Literature
3. Accounting
4. Political Science
5. Film

A. Crook
B. Dry Cleaning or Acupuncture
C. Blockbuster Video clerk
D. Accountant
E. Alcoholic high school teacher with a beard, working on unpublishable novel, prone to fits of depression and suicidal rage

Answers: 1B, 2E, 3D, 4A, 5C

Or, pick your major by what you actually *like* doing:

- Working with kids? Become a teacher
- Taking care of sick friends? Become a nurse
- Smoking a lot of pot? Become an environmentalist
- Getting your dick sucked? Become an adult film performer

Or, pick one of these majors if you want to score a hot chick:

- Design studies
- Psychology
- Elementary education
- Nursing
- Art history

29. It's Too Late to Change Your Major from Philosophy to Business

You didn't want to major in philosophy, but after taking six philosophy classes and with your parents on your case, you figured you'd just major in it for now while getting your generals out of the way before picking something more useful. But when you go to change majors you're told it's too late. Now you will be graduating with a degree in existentialism. Useless!

The WTF Approach to Graduating with a F*#!-ing Bullshit B.A.

➤ **OPTION #1:** *Get an MBA*

A bachelors in business is useless anyhow if you don't get a masters. So, don't worry about what's on your certificate, you can always go back to school for business later.

➤ **OPTION #2:** *Lie*

Just put down that you majored in business. Who is really going to doubt you? In fact, say you have an MBA while you're at it. Just make sure to read enough *Business for Dummies*-type books to pull it off.

► OPTION #3: *Go to Law School*

Studies show that students who studied history and philosophy end up making more money in the long run. Why? Because they have no choice except to go to law school. Become a lawyer; Lord knows we need more of them.

► OPTION #4: *Be a Philosopher*

There are still real philosophers out there, but they are few and far between. If you're not smart enough to be a great academic, then just wear a toga and philosophize on the corner.

> **NOTE:** Do yourself a favor and buy *The Little Bathroom Book of Philosophy.*

► OPTION #5: *Become a Nihilistic Businessperson*

If you want to be a cold-hearted corporate suit, study your nihilism and Nietzsche. Remember: *might makes right*, biatch!

WTF ABOUT TOWN

We had the privilege of talking to one of the most promising philosophers in the country. The following conversation ensued:

WTF: We heard that you are a philosopher.

Philosopher: Indeed, I am.

WTF: Is that your cardboard box? Do you live there?

Philosopher: That is a good question. Well, it certainly seems that way doesn't it? But how can we be sure that our senses are perceiving reality as it truly is? How, for instance, do you know that you are not dreaming this experience entirely? How, for instance, can you prove that these words "cardboard" and "box" are actual representations of real objects or just terms we used to differentiate certain visual "forms" that comprise our reality?

WTF: Interesting. We never thought if it that way.

Philosopher: Thank you. Now can I interest either of you in some crack?

COLLEGE IS NO LAUGHING MATTER

"I took a test in existentialism. I left all the answers blank and got 100."
—Woody Allen

30. Your Professor Asks You Out to Dinner

You have really been enjoying your political science class. Your professor seems to really like you, and you find her lectures simply fascinating. One day she asks you to stay after class to talk about your latest assignment. After telling you what a great paper it is and what a great writer you are, she asks you to come to dinner to "discuss it in greater detail." But you know what she's really asking for . . .

The WTF Approach to Handling a Horny F*#!-ing Prof

➤ OPTION #1: *Go and Try to Screw Her*

Bang the living shit out of her. If she is hot and you're single, then why not? Make sure you do her good though, you would hate for her to fail you for not being good in bed.

> **IF YOUR PROFESSOR IS A GUY . . .**
>
> Well, if you like dudes then go for it. If you *don't* like dudes, then go anyway for a free meal. Gays love good food.

➤ OPTION #2: *Go and Be Annoying*

If you aren't interested in the old bag, then go for a free meal and just annoy the shit out of her. Be the worst date ever. Talk about beer bongs and parties and the one time you drew a dick on your friend's forehead after he blacked out. She'll leave you alone after that for the rest of the semester.

➤ OPTION #3: *Don't Go*

You will need to come up with a good excuse, one that can't be argued. Like, you are on a strict liquid diet or you are agoraphobic and can barely make it to class.

for the ladies . . .

Go to dinner and start crying. Then explain you just broke up with your boyfriend—who happens to be a professional body builder—because he beat the shit out of some guy who was flirting with you. Then tell him you think you just started your period . . . at the table. If he has any sense, he won't even look at you after that, but he'll be sure to pass you.

COLLEGE KID QUOTE

"My professor is *so* hot; I wish he would totally ask me out!"

—Richard Gaylord, freshman at University of San Francisco

31. Your Girlfriend Has a Crush on Her Professor

She talks about him constantly—about how "smart" and "funny" he is, how he "knows everything," and how he has "really opened her eyes." Recently, you notice she's stopped referring to him as Professor Richard Long, Ph.D., and started calling him by his nickname, Dr. Dick. Not only that, she's also texted him several times about some "assignments" late into the night. Seems as if your girlfriend's professor has ignited her intellectual curiosity, and sparked a burning flame in her pants.

The WTF Approach to Squashing Your Girl's F*#!-ing Crush

➤ OPTION #1: *Spread Rumors about Him*

If your girl is getting too close, spread rumors that he has herpes or some other unfortunate sexually transmitted malady. When the grapevine gets to your girl, she'll be more than happy to keep her crush to the classroom and leave the bedroom just for you.

➤ OPTION #2: *Become Smart and Interesting—Quickly*

If you can become smarter and more interesting, maybe your girl won't have to chase her teachers to satisfy her intellectual needs. Stop working on your cardio and exercise your brain.

> **OPTION #3:** *Get Him Fired*

If things are really getting out of hand and you're sure it's only a matter of time before your girl ends up playing the skin flute with her music teacher, use any means necessary—fair and unfair—to get him the boot. Plant drugs in his office, pay one of his female students to accuse him of sexual harassment, or just beat him up so bad that he'll end up looking like Stephen Hawking. Because even with those kinds of smarts, when you look *that* bad, you don't get laid.

YOUR GIRL MIGHT HAVE A CRUSH ON HER PROFESSOR IF . . .
- ❏ She gets all dolled up before class—just his.
- ❏ She quotes him on a daily basis.
- ❏ She sits in on his other classes.
- ❏ She laughs at all his jokes.
- ❏ She's a little dirty whore and you *know* it.

IN THE FUTURE . . .

Research the professors that teach the classes your girlfriend is considering. Find out what they look like, if they are married, what their reputation and accomplishments are, and so on. If the course book says that the professor is TBA, whoever ends up teaching the class probably won't be an academic big shot and therefore shouldn't be a threat.

32. You Shit Your Pants in the Middle of a Presentation

You've finally gotten over your fear of public speaking and you're right in the middle of a big presentation that counts for half your grade. Things are going smoothly until you feel a familiar pain. Your stomach is churning and the gas is flowing. It hurts so bad that you can't take it anymore. You have to try and squeeze out a fart. You gently open your butt cheeks and try to sneakily let out some gas when you accidentally take a dump in your pants. Yes, you just sharted in front of the entire class. Congratulations.

The WTF Approach to Recovering from a F*#!-ing Shart

►OPTION #1: *Muddle Through, Literally*

If the smell isn't too bad, tough it out. As a baby, you used to sit in your own shit for hours. So finish your presentation, and then get the hell out of there.

►OPTION #2: *Yell "Fire!"*

People will immediately start to freak out and make their way to the door, allowing you to waddle off stage and clean up.

➤ OPTION #3: *Admit It*

Start out your presentation with: "Hey everyone, I just shit my pants." Not only will they not believe you, they will all start laughing. And every great speech should open with a good joke.

➤ OPTION #4: *Use It*

Pull your pants down and take out the shit. Make it part of your presentation. This is an extreme move we know, but at least your professor won't forget you or the presentation, nor can he deny your level of commitment to the class. You might never get laid again, but at least you'll get an A.

Depending on which class you're giving the presentation in, here's how you can use the crap to your advantage:

Biology: Talk about what the shit is made of and how it comes out of your ass.

Microbiology: Look at the shit under a microscope to see what it's *really* made of.

Physics: Throw the shit against the wall and record the velocity and consistency during flight.

Chemistry: Light the shit on fire.

History: Talk about the historical perspective of shit and its properties and how it has evolved from early civilization to modern times.

Philosophy: Is this shit really there? How do you know that for sure? Can you prove it?

Sociology: Discuss the social implications if you shoved this shit down your mouth in front of everyone.

Psychology: What would Freud say about "accidentally" shitting your pants in the middle of an important presentation?

33. You Can't Focus Because You're In Love with Your Professor

It's a common love story: student falls in love with teacher. Unfortunately, some teachers reciprocate the sentiment. When you registered for literature, you just thought it would be another old woman boring everyone to tears with her monotone lectures. But as it turns out, not only is your professor *not* old, she's an attractive and fascinating young woman. You go from thinking about what a great class this is to thinking about how great your professor is to thinking about how great your professor would be in the sack to thinking about how much you love her. Before you know it, you're head over heels for your professor and you *must* have her!

The WTF Approach to Releasing Your F*#!-ing Feelings

> ➤ STEP #1: *Find Another Girl and Role-Play*

Sometimes all you need is to do the deed; usually what you thought was love was nothing more than lust. So find a girl, dress her up like a professor (don't tell her about your crush), then play out a teacher-student scenario. A lot of girls find this hot. And, hey, if all goes well, you might just have found your dream girl.

➤ STEP #2: *Tell Her*

If getting off on the role-play didn't satisfy your needs, you should just come out and tell her that you can't stop thinking about her and you want to take her on a date. Odds are she will shoot you down, but that might only be because she doesn't want to lose her job. But trust us, it's good to start being honest with your feelings now.

➤ STEP #3: *Drop the Class*

You tried to replace her. You tried to reach out to her. But now you've been rejected. In most cases this is a one-way ticket to heartache and a restraining order. Get out while you still can.

TEACHER/STUDENT LOVE STORIES:

- *Notes on a Scandal*
- *Wild Things*
- *My Tutor*
- Every *Lifetime* movie of the week!

for the ladies . . .

If your professor is a dude and you're in love with him, then you are a little ho—he's twice your age!

Famous Teacher/Student Relationships

Debra Lafave, 35	14-year-old boy
Pamela Turner, 27	13-year-old boy
Pamela Smart, 22	15-year-old boy
Dennis Peterson, 50	Several teenage girls
Toni Pala Blilie, 45	14-year-old student
Edward Fischer, 40	Thirty-nine young boys!
Beth Friedman, 42	15-year-old boy

34. You Get an Erection During Your Physics Presentation

There you are in front of a large classroom explaining how the force of one object can affect the space of another. Now you're not sure if it's the fact that you're really nervous or if it's the girl with the big tits that you've been eyeing all semester, but suddenly you can't focus. In fact, the force of something is definitely affecting the space of something else. You are getting a raging hard-on in your jeans and there is no way to stop it.

The WTF Approach to Welcoming F*#!-ing Unexpected Wood

➤ OPTION #1: *Get Creative*

When an actress on television is pregnant in real life but her character isn't pregnant on the show, the writers find a way to conceal the baby bump. Your bump should be much easier to hide. No offense. Stand in front of the desk. Turn your back to the class, or hold a book over your crotch. Then think of Rosie O'Donnell bent over covered in margarine and pray it goes away.

➤ OPTION #2: *Use It*

Point it out. Explain that this is part of your presentation: to show how something *so* large can expand

and contract in such a confined space. Maybe McTitty in the front row will want to conduct her own experiment after seeing it.

➤ OPTION #3: *Jerk Off in Class*

Hey, this is the most surefire way to get rid of it. It probably won't take you long. Aim at McTitty. That will teach her to wear tight T-shirts without a bra—and teach the class about projectiles.

for the ladies . . .

This may not seem like it's something to worry about, but having hard nipples can also be very embarrassing and distracting. Wear band aides over the areola.

Erection Equation

$$\frac{\text{Mass of tits} \times \text{Mass of dick}}{\text{Speed of blood flow}} = \text{Erection}$$

THOUGHTS THAT KILL AN ERECTION:

- Dead kittens
- Your grandmother (unless she's a cougar)
- Michael Moore
- Michael Jackson
- Colonoscopies
- Nipple hair
- Nipple hair on Holocaust victims
- Cankles
- That birth video from health class
- Photos of STDs
- AIDS
- A dead baby sandwich on rye, with that mustard that you *hate*

IN THE FUTURE . . .

The next time you have to stand in front of a large group of people, wear a cup.

35. You Are the Only Creationist in Your Science Class

The earth was created billions of years ago. Human beings evolved over millions of years from lesser primates. The earth was once inhabited by giant creatures called dinosaurs. *Can you believe this nonsense?* What heresy! Don't these people know that an invisible, all powerful God created the earth in six days and then took a break on Sunday? Read your Bible, professor.

The WTF Approach to Reconciling with Your F*#!-ing Faith

➤ OPTION #1: *Find a Clever Way to Make Peace Between Scripture and Science*

Say that a "day" in biblical terms could have meant a billion years. This way (even though it's complete bullshit) you can resolve the gaping contradiction between reality and Genesis without sacrificing your faith.

➤ OPTION #2: *Transfer Schools*

Did you *really* think Berkeley would be for you? Go to a school with like-minded students who would rather watch a baptism than go skinny dipping with the women's volleyball team.

Science is not a religion. Sure, scientists often take certain principles of the universe to be gospel, only later to reject them when they're disproved, but this fact just reinforces the way in which science is distinct from religion. Scientific doctrine, unlike religious doctrine, is subject to change.

Religious fundamentalists love to question the legitimacy of science as a method of discovering truth simply because certain "scientific truths" are sometimes later proven false. "Science gets things wrong all the time; they're just theories," say the creationists. These people need to take their eyes off their Bible for a second and look around. Cell phones, computers, rockets, airplanes, cars, medicine, vibrating sexual objects—we're surrounded by science everyday, science that has produced tangible results—real things in the world. It seems absurd that a creationist can talk on a cell phone, visit a doctor, and take an airplane, but then discredit science the minute they step in a geology class.

➤ OPTION #3: *Stop Being a Moron*

Join the rest of the Western world and accept evolution. It's scary to be a heretic, we know, but just think how much better you'll feel when you turn to drinking, drugs, and the occasional abortion to cheer you up, like all your peers.

➤ OPTION #4: *Die*

Why stay in this life when there is a better one waiting for you, right?

Creationism as a "Science"

Please. A scientific theory must be proven; it requires evidence. What is the evidence for creationism, a collection of Jewish short stories and the occasional citing of the Virgin Mary in a grilled cheese sandwich?

It doesn't matter if you can prove there was a Flood. This is what creationists and religious fundamentalists that take the Bible literally don't get: Even if certain events depicted in the Bible have been proven true, it doesn't mean that the biblical explanations of those events is therefore also true. For centuries scholars dismissed Homer's epic tale of Troy and the Trojan War as pure legend. Then in 1868, a German self-taught archaeologist named Heinrich Schliemann excavated what is now accepted to be the ancient city. So now that we know there really is a Troy and that Homer was telling the truth, are we also to believe in nymphs, gods, cyclopses, and that the whole thing was fought over a hot chick? Of course not. Same logic applies. Some scientists now believe that there actually was a terrible deluge in the ancient world, but that fact doesn't mean that an invisible god told a 700-year-old Jewish man named Noah to gather up all the animals he could and then coax them to fuck on his boat.

POP QUIZ

Which of the following groups accept creationism as described in Genesis?

A. Jews
B. Muslims
C. Christians
D. Dipshits
E. All of the Above

Answer: E

WTFACT: According to a 2000 poll:

- 20 percent of Americans believe public schools should teach evolution only
- 17 percent of Americans believe that only evolution should be taught in science classes—religious explanations should be taught in another class
- 29 percent of Americans believe that creationism should be discussed in science class as a "belief" not a scientific theory
- 13 percent of Americans believe that creationism and evolution should be taught as "scientific theories" in science class
- 16 percent of Americans believe that only creationism should be taught

NOTE: While we cannot ensure that these numbers are 100 percent accurate, we can assure you of one fact: Americans are completely out of their fucking minds.

36. You're the Only Guy in Your Women's Studies Class

When you signed up for women's studies you thought it would be a class about how chicks think. You figured you would learn how to get into their heads so you can score. But on the first day of class you realize what kind of hell you've just stepped into. You're surrounded by a mob of angry, embittered women looking for a face to blame.

The WTF Approach to Surviving a Class Filled with Angry F*#!-ing Chicks

➤ **OPTION #1: *Use It***

Just because these girls hate men, doesn't mean that they don't need dick. Being the only dude in class might have its advantages.

➤ **OPTION #2: *Come Clean***

Tell everyone you're considering a sex change and since you will one day be the proud owner of a vagina you really wanted to learn everything you can about your future gender's history.

➤ **OPTION #3: *Divide and Conquer***

Get the women to hate one another despite their feigned solidarity in class by starting vicious rumors. Turn these so called feminists into the real yentas that they are. Sit back and laugh as the claws come out.

POP QUIZ

Which is the best way to score with a girl?

A. *Guy:* Hi
   Girl: Hello.
   Guy: You up for some fuckin'?
B. *Guy:* Hey.
   Girl: Hello.
   Guy: You know I have always admired Elizabeth Blackwell
   Girl: Who?
   Guy: She was the first female doctor. She overcame taunts and prejudice while at medical school and graduated at the top of her class.
   Girl: Wow.
   Guy: So you up for some fuckin'?

Answer: B

WTFACT: Studies show that groups of women who spend a lot of time together begin to experience the same menstrual cycles. If you think women's studies class is bad normally, avoid every third week.

COLLEGE IS NO LAUGHING MATTER

"You don't appreciate a lot of stuff in school until you get older. Little things like being spanked every day by a middle aged woman: Stuff you pay good money for in later life."—Emo Philips

IN THE FUTURE . . .

Read the class description carefully before you sign up.

37. You Have to Complete Your Foreign Language Requirement . . . and the Only Available Course Is Swahili

You didn't want to take a foreign language. Why should you anyway? Everyone speaks English—or should. The English conquered the world so that we Americans wouldn't have to learn another language. WTF? Despite this truth, college is college, and it has its requirements. You knew you should have signed up earlier so you could take Italian, French, or another romance language that might help get you chicks. But you waited until the last day and now the only language available is Swahili. Swa-fuckin-hili! Now what?

The WTF Approach to Making the Most of F*#!-ing Course Requirements

➤ STEP #1: *Become a Swahili Expert*

The more obscure the discipline, the easier it is to become an expert. If you study hard enough, you'll be the best Swahili speaker on campus, and you might just secure yourself a job translating or teaching in the future. In this shit economy, developing a very unique and specific skill is your best bet—no matter how useless it appears on paper.

➤ STEP #2: *Move to East Africa*

Swahili is spoken in much of East Africa as well as the Democratic Republic of the Congo, and it is the official language of Uganda, Tanzania, and Kenya. It's the first language for about 10 million Africans and the second language of around 80 million.

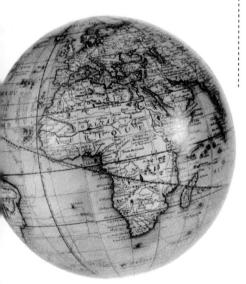

Just think of how easy it will be to score with an East African chick. They're literally *starving* for your attention.

Swahili Proverbs

Every culture has words of wisdom to impart with the rest of the world. Here are some of the greatest proverbs from Swahili speaking peoples:

Atakae hachoki:

A person in need never gets tired.

Akipenda chongo huita kengeza:

A person in love with a one-eyed person calls her/him "cross-eyed."

Fadhila za punda ni mateke:

The way a donkey expresses gratitude is by giving someone a bunch of kicks. (This should come in handy!)

38. You See Your Professor at a Party Doing Drugs

Is that him? You look across the room and see what looks like your professor burying his face in a bong like a gopher in a hole. No, it can't be you say. But when the smoke clears you see his face clearly. It *is* him. Your professor is really smoking pot and doing God knows what else at a party. What to do?

The WTF Approach to Partying with Your F*#!-ing Professor

➤ **OPTION #1: *Join Him***

If your professor is doing drugs, then obviously it's okay. Take this opportunity to bond with him. Ask him questions about the class material so he thinks you find it interesting. Then again, if you smoke enough, it might actually become interesting.

for the ladies . . .

Now is your chance to hit on him. You've always wanted to but it was just never the right situation. He's feeling good and he wants to feel better. Just walk up to him and say something sexy like: "Hi there, professor. Is that a gun under your corduroy jacket or are you just happy to see me?" It works every time.

➤ OPTION #2: *Blackmail Him*

Threaten to tell his wife if he has one (though she is probably the same kind of dope-smoking left-wing hippie that he is), or threaten to get him canned. You could also try to shake him down for cash, but he's obviously broke if he's a teacher. Better to just blackmail him into giving you that desperately needed A.

➤ OPTION #3: *Get Him to Get You Laid*

Ask him to introduce you to one of his groupies at the party. Any professor who likes to party has got plenty of poon to spare.

39. Someone Cheats Off You During the Final Exam

You've been studying hard the last couple of weeks for finals. So hard, in fact, that you have cut down to ten beers a day. True, they were 40-ounce beers, but still. The point is that you were making an effort and it paid off. You totally aced it. And so did the kid next to you—though not because he studied. You thought you saw him looking at your test, but you were too busy concentrating to be sure. It was only when that freckle-faced prick got his exam back with the same grade you did that it was undeniably clear: He cheated.

The WTF Approach to Dealing with a F*#!-ing Cheat

➤ OPTION #1: *Tattle*

Why should this lazy prick get the same grade you did when you were studying all night while he sat on his ass? Don't let him get away with it. Tell the professor that you absolutely saw your neighbor cheating off you. Make sure to add that you feel bad doing this but that it isn't "fair" since you worked so hard. The professor will still probably think that you're a little tattle-tale pussy, but so be it.

➤ OPTION #2: *Let It Go*

Don't be such a hard ass. It's not like his cheating affects your grade—unless, of course, your professor grades on a curve. In that case, go with Option #3.

➤ OPTION #3: *Beat the Shit Out of Him*

Grab him by the collar after class and slam him into the wall. Make him confess to his sins and then, when he does, beat him up some more. This will not change anything, but it will make you feel good (assuming that you are a sick fuck).

➤ OPTION #4: *Blackmail Him*

What good is it to tattle like a baby or to beat him up? Maybe it's best that, instead, you make him give you something for cheating off you. Quid pro quo.

Things to Consider Before Telling on the Cheater

Before you go and tattle on or blackmail your cheating class-mate, you might want to factor in a few things. Sometimes it's good to keep your mouth shut, not out of principle, but to save your ass. Consider:

- Height, weight, and muscle density of the cheater
- Ethnic background of the cheater; don't mess with the Irish—they'll beat your ass.
- The cheater's shoes: you can tell how rich or poor a man is by his shoes. If he's wearing sneakers from Target, don't bother blackmailing because he doesn't have any loot. And don't tell on him either. Let the poor schmuck off the hook.

NOTE: Converse sneakers are neutral. They don't tell anything about your cheater's financial status, since everyone and their mother now wears them. In this event, look at his watch.

Chapter 4

Flunked!

40. You Get Caught Cheating and Are Thrown Out of Class

You were caught cheating. And you can't deny it by saying that you have some sort of crossed-eyed problem that makes it seem like you are staring at your neighbor's paper. No, the professor caught you with the notes written on your desk—and this is the first exam he's given out. No excuses. No bull. You've been caught red-handed . . . now what?

The WTF Approach to Beating the F*#!-ing Cheating Rap

►OPTION #1: *Give a Sob Story*

Go to his office and beg him to let you retake the exam. Tell him you couldn't study because your mom died or that you just found out over the weekend that you had AIDS—not HIV but full-blown AIDS . . . you have six months to live. Make sure that if you are going to conjure up a sob story to explain your being a cheater, that it is as devastatingly sad as the aforementioned stories. Everyone has a dead grandma and has gotten the flu—don't go there. Go the dead mom or the AIDS route and cry like a baby. Even the coldest, by-the-book professors will crack and give you a break.

➤ OPTION #2: *Bribe Him*

Offer him money to forget about the whole thing. If he accepts, offer him more to just go ahead and give you an A.

➤ OPTION #3: *Change Your Major*

What were you doing studying biology anyway? Now that you know you're a sneaky, cheating liar with no integrity whatsoever, change your major from pre-med to pre-law. You'll do wonderfully.

➤ OPTION #4: *Compromise*

If your professor is too square for a bribe and doesn't give a shit about your sad life, then try and convince him to just fail you and not bring it to the dean's attention.

BEST WAYS TO CHEAT—AND GET AWAY WITH IT:

Get a cast: Break your arm if you must, but just make sure you get a cast. Get people to sign it and then write the information for the test in between the signatures.

Get a doctor's note: Have your doctor say that you have a bladder issue and need to urinate frequently. Make sure to inform your teachers at the beginning of the semester that you *must* go to the bathroom every ten minutes. This will make it easy for you to check your notes during test time while you're in the john.

Write the answers on your baseball cap: Jot the information on the inside of a baseball cap's bill. During the exam, take the cap off and place it in front of you upside down for easy viewing.

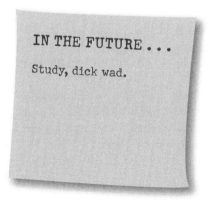

IN THE FUTURE . . .

Study, dick wad.

41. Your Professor Is Out to Fail You

Your friends think you're paranoid, your parents think you're lying, but you know it's the truth. Your professor hates you and is out to fail you for no good reason. Maybe you remind him of someone—a bully from high school, a mean uncle, or that jerk in the blue pickup truck who knocked up his daughter—whatever the reason, you're on his naughty list and you just can't seem to get off.

The WTF Approach to Getting Around a F*#!-ing Professor Out to Get You

➤ STEP #1: *Drop the Class*

Even if it's past the date to drop, you can still drop it for an incomplete. While an incomplete sucks, it beats failing. Retake the class at another time with another professor who isn't a prick.

➤ STEP #2: *Pucker Up*

If an incomplete means you won't graduate—or worse, get tossed from the school—you're going to have to kiss some ass, big shot. Bring a new shiny red apple to class every day, and if that doesn't work offer to suck him off.

➤ STEP #3: *Poison the Apple*

Put a little arsenic in the apple every day until he chokes on his own spit and leaves this world forever—double the dosage come finals just to make sure.

> **NOTE:** While we here at *WTF* want to see you succeed, we don't want to see you go to prison. (Eh, maybe we do.) Keep in mind that believe it or not, homicide does look worse on a resume than a failing grade in biology.

for the ladies . . .

Based on what you have read of this book so far, what do you think our advice is to you? We'll give you three options:

A. Spread your legs.

B. Spread them wider.

C. Attach your ankles to your ears.

Yes. The answer is C. Wow, you're getting so smart!

42. You Can't Stop Falling Asleep in Class

You thought that you could party all night and still be alert enough to take copious notes during psych class. But these all-nighters are starting to wear you down. You know that you should stay in and study instead of chug beer and take body shots off a freshman coed's tanned abs, but you just can't seem to stay away from the fun. Luckily, we at *WTF* can help. Here's a crash-course on how to stop turning your desk into a puddle of drool and your professor against you.

The WTF Approach to Handling the F*#!-ing Classroom Zzzs

➤ OPTION #1: *Party in Class*

Rather than stay up all night partying, take the party to the lecture hall. Top off half a bottle of Pepsi with some rum. This way you can have all the fun you would at a party, while still being an enthusiastic participant in class (perhaps a little too enthusiastic). The pro-fessor will love you and so will your classmates . . . if you share!

➤ OPTION #2: *Break Down and Start Crying*

If your grade is in jeopardy, force a tear and tell your professor that you haven't slept well because you've been spending all your nights at the hospital, where your poor girlfriend hovers between life and death. Make sure to know a hospital offhand so you can be specific, which will make your lie more believable.

PROFESSOR TIP: To perfect the crying game, make sure to take an acting class early in your college career—you're going to need those lying skills to make it through the next four years.

➤ OPTION #3: *Think Fast*

If you're called out for dozing off, explain to your professor that you have been practicing the art of meditation . . . very Eckhart Tolle. This *is* the way you absorb your material.

➤ OPTION #4: *Say You're a Narcoleptic*

Tell the professor you have a slight case of narcolepsy. If he believes you, now you have an open invitation to fall asleep in class whenever you want.

for the ladies . . .

If you sleepy ladies are reprimanded by a male professor for constantly dozing off, you might want to tell him (again, with tears) that financial troubles have forced you to take a night job as a stripper, which has ruined your sleeping patterns. As you tell this sad story, be sure to gently sway back and forth in a progressively seductive manner. Your professor will be so turned on and saddened at the same time he won't know what to do—except cut you a break.

43. You Have a Paper Due Tomorrow That You Haven't Started

You have always been a procrastinator, but usually it all turns out okay. You can study the night before an exam and still ace the test. No problem. But this time you really screwed up, and there's no way to wing it. You know that big paper that's worth half your grade? Well, it's due tomorrow and you haven't even begun.

The WTF Approach to Finishing a F*#!-ing Paper by Deadline

➤ OPTION #1: *Sit Down and Write It*

If you sit down with a few hundred Red Bulls and double-shot lattes you should be able to bang it out. Writing papers is easy. Just make sure your thesis is clear and then prove your point. If you don't have time to write real transitions between ideas, just keep using words like "furthermore," "in addition," "also," and such. Furthermore, use a lot of quotes to take up lines. In addition, make sure to draw attention to the subjective nature of paper grading by using phrases like "in my opinion," "it is my contention," and so on. Also, make the font as big as you can without being too conspicuous.

➤ OPTION #2: *Buy One*

If you've ever been on the Internet, you probably already know this type of service is available. There are several sites that offer term papers for sale on just about every subject. We suggest finding one that charges a monthly membership fee and then splitting the cost with your roommate or a friend. Of course, if you go with this option, you will never really learn anything, but when have you ever learned anything from writing a paper that you didn't forget by next semester?

➤ OPTION #3: *Steal One*

Hack into a classmate's computer and take his paper. Destroy his hard drive so he has no record of it. While you may not learn anything, you will be teaching your classmate a valuable lesson about trusting others.

➤ OPTION #4: *Get Your Girlfriend to Write It for You*

Tell your girlfriend that you had a wildly romantic night planned for her but you have to cancel because of this damn paper. She knows how slow you type. Odds are she will offer to help, and by help, we mean she'll do all the work. Grab a bottle of wine and get loaded while she types away. Then bang her as her reward. If you don't have a girlfriend, find one fast. That's what they're for, anyway.

> **COLLEGE KID QUOTE**
>
> "I once had this paper due and I was like, oh shit, it's like the night before. And then I like totally didn't have time and failed the class."
>
> —Wayne Smith, *still* a freshman at University of Arizona online (he's 28)

The WTF Sample Paper

Most term papers follow the same structure and format, which means you can get a jump on the one you didn't start by using this template. By inserting a few pieces of key information and making a few choices between the supplied choices, you'll have one hell of paper.

While researching _____ it is clear that
[insert: subject, book title, or article title]

the main _____ is intended as a metaphor for
[choose: idea, theme, or bullshit]

_____. This is symbolic because it represents a
[choose: life, death, or existential woe]

classic case of man versus _____. The questions
[choose: man, nature, or society]

raised by author are _____. In my
[choose: controversial, profound, or who-gives-a-shit?]

opinion, this _____ novel focuses on the struggle
[choose: classic, brilliant, or lame-ass]

of the individual to maintain his _____
[choose: identity, humanity, need to feel like a big shot]

in the modern world. In conclusion, I found _____
[insert: subject, book title, or article title]

to be one of the most moving examples of the natural human desire to

give life _____. The End.
[choose: meaning, purpose, or . . . God this is fucking boring!]

44. You're the Dumbest Kid in All Your Classes

They say it is better to be a big fish in a little pond than a little fish in a big pond. Perhaps you should have thought over that expression a little more before deciding to go to a school that you knew should not have accepted you. It looks good on your resume to graduate from a fancy school, but it doesn't look that great if you barely get by. You just weren't Yale material. Don't feel bad, there have been others in the same boat—a recent U.S. president comes to mind . . .

The WTF Approach to Surviving as the F*#!-ing Stupid Kid

➤ OPTION #1: *Switch to an Easier Major*

If you are in the Ivy League when you should be in community college, you're going to have to get off that pre-med track. It's the only way to shine academically and stop embarrassing yourself. To stay at the top, pick from the left field of academic majors. Choose a major like drama, art, or sociology.

➤ OPTION #2: *Downgrade Schools*

In a less prestigious school, you'll not only perform better, you'll have more fun too. When you're getting As on tests and blowjobs between classes, you'll forget all about your former school.

➤ OPTION #3: *Ignorance Is Bliss*

Okay, you're the dumbest kid in class. Who cares? Keep a low profile and your mouth shut so you don't make a jackass out of yourself. Study hard and you'll graduate, not with honors or the respect of your peers, but graduate nonetheless. Remember, you'll never have to see these pricks again—unless you're fixing their office's elevator.

How to Pass—When You're a Moron

Here's how to handle questions when you don't know the answer, as well as how *not* to handle them.

WHAT TO SAY . . .

Question: What is your take on the situation in Kashmir?
Answer: That is such a complicated issue. I don't even know where to start. But *something* has to be done.

Question: What do you think should be done about Darfur?
Answer: I think I'm in the majority here. What's *your* take?

Question: How should the government handle the current economic crisis?
Answer: Well, it certainly is a crisis. And therefore should be dealt with as such.

WHAT *NOT* TO SAY . . .

Question: What is your take on the situation in Kashmir?
Answer: I don't even wear cashmere. It sheds.

Question: What do you think should be done about Darfur?
Answer: I don't believe in cruelty to animals. I don't care what kind of fur it is.

Question: How should the government handle the current economic crisis?
Answer: What crisis?

45. You Choose to Plagiarize So You Can Party . . . and Then Get Caught

It's the night before your mid-term essay is due. You put it off forever and now you have no choice but to buckle down. But then you hear about this amazing party . . . shit! You go online to look up some resources—wow, these people really know what they're talking about—and so you decide to just copy their thoughts. A week later, your professor calls you in to talk about plagiarism. Thief! Maybe it wasn't such a good idea . . .

The WTF Approach to Talking Your Way Out of F*#!-ing Plagiarism Charges

➤ OPTION #1: *State Your Case*

Explain that these are also your ideas and that great minds think—and sometimes write—*exactly* alike. If he doesn't buy it, offer to write the paper again. Then pay a really smart kid to write if for

you. In fact, that's what you should have done in the first place. You deserve to be caught, dumbass!

➤ OPTION #2: *Lie*

Admit that you used other people's work but forgot to attach your sources. If you copied word for word, you'll have to say that you accidentally turned in a rough draft of your paper. Go home and quickly pull up the material you ripped off, change the words around, and list them on your works cited page.

➤ OPTION #3: *Flip the Switch*

That's right; tell this professor he is insulting you as an academic and that you will not be accused of something so outrageous. Then drop the class and file a complaint. Don't go too far, however, or they might call your bluff and actually read your paper.

IN THE FUTURE . . .

Buy a paper online.

The WTF Guide to Good Plagiarizing

Learn how to copy, dipshit!

Text to Copy

COLLEGE KID QUOTE

" I'm glad I'm not bisexual. I couldn't stand being rejected by men as well as women. "

—Bernard Manning

The Wrong Way to Copy

I'm glad I'm not bisexual. Because, I couldn't stand being rejected by men as well as women.

The Right Way

You see I could never be bisexual. I couldn't stand getting rejections from both sexes.

HOW TO WRITE A PAPER:

1. Sit at your desk.
2. Read over the assignment carefully to make certain you understand it.
3. Walk down to the vending machines and buy some Red Bull.
4. Stop at your friend's room.
5. Talk about banging chicks and *Family Guy*.
6. Go back to your room and sit back at your desk.
7. Read over the assignment again to make absolutely certain you understand it.
8. Check your e-mail; reply to everyone who sent you a message.
9. Check your cell phone; return any missed calls and texts.
10. Go take a shit.
11. Check your e-mail again.
12. Watch porn on your computer.
13. Whack off to that hot girl from Bio class.
14. Nap.
15. Eat.
16. Read over the assignment again.
17. Check your e-mail to make sure no one sent you any urgent messages since the last time you checked your e-mail.
18. Watch *Family Guy*.
19. Look through your roommate's personal stuff.
20. Sit down and do some serious thinking about your plans for the future.
21. Decide what kind of super powers you would want if you were on *Heroes*.
22. Read over the assignment one more time, just for the hell of it.
23. Whack off to the *other* hot girl from Bio class.
24. Lie face down on the floor and moan.
25. Type the paper.

46. You Pull an All-Nighter and Still Aren't Prepared for the Final Exam

Every semester it's the same story. "I've got time," you say. "Finals aren't until the end of the semester. I'll just have to really hit the books a couple weeks before." Then a couple weeks become a couple days and now it's only a couple hours. It's the night before and you're freaking out in the middle of an all-nighter. You're just not ready.

The WTF Approach to Making It Through the F*#!-ing Exam

➤ OPTION #1: *Sit Next to a Smart Kid and Cheat*

That's what they're there for, right? If you were smart you would have picked a seat next to this kid early on so it wouldn't look weird the day of the exam, but then again if you were that smart you would be the smart kid and not the loser sitting next to him.

➤ OPTION #2: *Pull the Fire Alarm*

Right before you head in to the class, pull the alarm. Everyone will have to exit. When they do, grab a test and start looking up the answers. It will take a while before everyone is allowed back in. Class might even get canceled and now you have the test. Score. You can sell it to your classmates and cash in.

➤ OPTION #3: *Drink Ipecac*

Ipecac's a liquid designed to make you instantly puke, usually reserved for mothers to give their little kids if they swallow poison. Right before you walk in, take a swig and then puke all over the desk. The professor will have to excuse you, giving you some more time to study.

WTF: UP CLOSE AND PERSONAL

As I've confessed already, I wasn't exactly the greatest high school student. In fact, I sucked. I sucked so bad that in order to graduate, I needed an A on my senior project, which included a paper and a speech about the paper. I aced the paper. Whew. Next was the speech. But on the day in question I wasn't ready. What the fuck would I do? I decided to do what any student serious about graduating would do: I went to the drugstore and bought ipecac.

When it was time for my speech, I went around the corner, took a big swig, and came back in class. Within thirty seconds I vomited all over the bag of the redhead girl next to me. Heading for the door and covering my mouth, I continued to vomit violently through my fingers. And I mean *violently*. By the time I was finished, the school bathroom looked like it had hosted a food fight.

As I waited for a friend's mom to pick me up, lying in a pool of my own barf, my teacher had the audacity to ask if I would be okay enough to do my speech. I just glared at him through the globs of puke hanging from my eyelids. He got the message. He told me that he would make a rare exception and go against school policy by letting me make it up. A couple days later—and just twenty-four hours before graduation—I did just that. And yes, I got an A!

—GB

47. You Overslept and Missed Your Mid-Term

The alarm goes off and you hit Snooze and think, just ten more minutes. When it goes off again, you turn it off and think, I'll count to sixty and get up. 1, 2, 3, 4 . . . The next thing you know you wake up an hour later. Shit, you missed class, and what's worse, you had your mid-term today. WTF?

The WTF Approach to Recovering from F*#!-ing Oversleeping

➤ OPTION #1: *Just Make Something Up*

Go see your professor and tell her the electricity went out in your room and your alarm never went off. Then beg her to let you take a makeup exam. Not quite the truth, but there will be no way for your professor to prove you wrong. Just be prepared if she asks you to take the exam right then and there.

➤ OPTION #2: *Fess Up*

Go see your professor and confess. Honesty is the best policy. Explain that you were up all night studying and that you just couldn't get yourself out of bed. While she probably won't let you make up the exam, at least you'll know you did the right thing. Lame ass.

➤OPTION #3: *Call in a Bomb Threat*

You will have to do it from a land-line so no one can trace it back to you. The classroom and building will be evacuated and class will be canceled. You're not only saving yourself, you're also helping out those who didn't study for the exam. You're a hero. Whoo-hoo!

➤OPTION #4: ~~Blow Up the Building~~

While it would get the job done, it's a bit drastic. And you'd probably get thrown in jail. If you think college exams are horrible, try giving an oral presentation to Bubba every night before bed.

IN THE FUTURE . . .

Take Adderall. That shit will keep you up for days. You'll be so wired you'll have to study. Substitutes for Adderall include crack cocaine, crystal meth, and intravenous Red Bull.

48. You Partied Too Much and Failed Out of School

Maybe it was the booze, maybe it was the drugs, or maybe you're just a fucking idiot who was destined for failure; whatever the reason, you are now in the middle of a collegiate catastrophe. You just received a letter asking you not to come back next semester due to your academic performance. As in, you've failed, flunked, get no college degree at all (sorry, figured we'd spell it out for a moron like you).

The WTF Approach to Life after F*#!-ing Flunking

➤ OPTION #1: *Welcome to Wal-Mart*

Without a college degree in this country your fate is sealed. Get a job working at Wal-Mart and just wait to pass away.

➤ OPTION #2: *Work on a Fishing Boat in Alaska*

Because it sucks really, really bad, just about anyone can get a job on a fishing boat off the coast of Alaska for a surprisingly good pay—around $1,500 per week.

➤ OPTION #3: *Steal a Smart Kid's Identity*

Make sure this kid is a total loser so that no one misses him after you off him. Take over his life, get a great job, marry a hot chick, and call it a day.

➤ OPTION #4: *Jerk Off*

Why not? You've obviously masturbated your academic career away anyhow. Might as well go back to doing what you do best.

HISTORY'S FAMOUS FAILURES:

Abraham Lincoln went to war a captain and returned a private. Afterward, he was a failure as a businessman. After that he was shot in the head.

Albert Einstein's childhood grades were so poor that his parents thought he was mentally handicapped. Turns out they were just typical overly critical Jewish parents.

Winston Churchill failed sixth grade. He was subsequently defeated in every election for public office until he became Prime Minister at the age of sixty-two. He later wrote, "Never give in, never give in, never, never, never, give up." Churchill finally did give up on January 24, 1965 when he forever left this world. Hypocrite.

Sigmund Freud was booed from the podium when he first presented his ideas to the scientific community of Europe. A strict Freudian, he still charged the attendees for the full hour.

Charles Darwin once said, "I was considered by all my masters and my father, a very ordinary boy, rather below the common standard of intellect." Ironically, the same thing can be said of anyone today who still doesn't believe his theories.

Thomas Edison's teachers said he was "too stupid to learn anything." He tried 9,000 experiments before he invented the light bulb, inspiring the famous joke opener: "How many experiments does it take to develop a light bulb . . ."

Adolf Hitler tried to kill every Jew. He failed too.

Chapter 5

Party Time

49. Your Parents Make a Surprise Visit and You're Drunk

"Surprise! We were just driving through and thought we would drop in!" And boy did they. Unfortunately you're wasted and what's worse, your parents are very religious and do not believe in the consumption of alcohol. You try to think fast but the four beers and three shots of tequila you slammed down in the last ten minutes are making it very difficult.

The WTF Approach to Enduring a F*#!-ing Unexpected Drop-In

➤ OPTION #1: *Play Sick*

Quickly run to the bathroom and pretend you are getting sick, and if you really drank a lot, you might not even have to pretend. Then crawl in bed and explain that you really need to get some sleep. Hopefully your parents will leave so you can get back to the party.

➤ OPTION #2: *Lie*

Tell them you were participating in a class project for a science class that monitors the effects of alcohol in your blood stream over a certain period of time. You know drinking is wrong, but this was for school and you want to excel.

➤ OPTION #3: *Blame It on Your Roommate*

Tell them he must have slipped some vodka into your Red Bull and you had no idea. This was not your fault, and you feel violated.

➤ OPTION #4: *Admit It*

Tell them you're drunk and proud of it. This is college, and you want to have fun while getting an education. What are they going to do, ground you?

➤ OPTION #5: *Make It a Party*

Break out a case a beer and get your parents wasted too. Explain to them that while you appreciate their views on the consumption of alcohol, even Jesus drank wine now and again.

WHAT THE F*#! DID HE SAY?

"You're not drunk if you can lie on the floor without holding on."—Joe E. Lewis

"I may be drunk, Miss, but in the morning I will be sober and you will still be ugly."—Winston Churchill

"Always do sober what you said you'd do drunk. That will teach you to keep your mouth shut."—Ernest Hemingway

"I feel sorry for people who don't drink. When they wake up in the morning, that's as good as they're gonna feel all day"—Frank Sinatra

"It takes only one drink to get me drunk. The trouble is, I can't remember if it's the thirteenth or the fourteenth."—George Burns

50. You Get Caught Using Your Fake ID

Your heart is pounding, your palms are sweating, you feel dizzy, and you haven't even had a drink yet. This bouncer is just not buying that the skinny white kid in front of him is Ahmed Karim. He has your fake ID and he's calling your bluff.

The WTF Approach to Using a F*#!-ing Fake

➤ STEP #1: *Stand Your Ground*

Even if you're shitting your pants, keep up the front that you're Ahmed. Don't back down. Start rattling off the license info. If you're smart, you memorized every detail of that fake ID, Ahmed.

➤ STEP #2: *Make a Scene*

That's right. Scream out, "This is ridiculous!" Then say that you have been here plenty of times and insist to see the manager. Tell the bouncer that you're going to get his ass fired. This is a risky move, but we have seen it work several times.

> **PROFESSOR TIP:** The more of an obnoxious prick you are, the more willing people are to believe you.

➤ STEP #3: *Play It Cool*

If making a scene didn't work in your favor, there is a chance that this bouncer will now call the cops. So calm down and start making a graceful exit.

➤ STEP #4: *Lie*

Tell him you know that it's not you. You found it on the ground and you were only kidding when you tried to use it. You wanted to be a good citizen and return it. Then spilt.

WTF: UP CLOSE AND PERSONAL

I was not only the owner of several fake IDs while I was at college, I also made them. I was very popular. They worked in every bar except one, Rudy's. This was one of those bars where the doormen have special bullshit-detecting powers, and if they caught you using a fake ID, they would sound a loud fog horn, turn off the music in the bar, and announce to everyone that you were just caught using a fake. Then they would take a Polaroid of you looking mortified and hang it up with the other underage losers. Not a risk I was ever willing to take. Some bars are worth the wait.

—JM

51. Your Favorite Band's Playing on Campus but Tickets Are Sold Out

You've downloaded every one of their songs to your iPod; you quote their lyrics when out with friends; you sing their songs in the shower (when you do shower)—they're your favorite band, and they're coming to your college. You can't wait to go . . . but then tickets sold out in about two minutes.

The WTF Approach to Getting to See the F*#!-ing Show

➤ OPTION #1: *Scalp*

If you have the cash, use it. Post a want ad on craigslist or Facebook that you're looking for tickets. Chances are someone will have to bail on the concert last minute and need the money.

➤ OPTION #2: *Steal*

Talk to some of your fellow students on campus, but no one you are good friends with. Find out who has tickets, then break into their room and steal them. It's every man for himself.

➤ OPTION #3: *Win Tickets*

A certain number of tickets are given away to radio stations—even the campus one—to help promote the show. They are usually front-row seats, so it might be worth your time to try and call in to win.

➤ OPTION #4: *Dress Like a Fireman*

Get your hands on an authentic fireman's uniform, then go to the venue and explain you need to do a safety check. Make sure you use words like "code," "emergency," and "fire exit." Once inside, hide out somewhere until the show starts.

NOTE: Women love men in uniform almost as much as they love band members. Hang on to that costume. You could end up getting some serious ass using it.

for the ladies
Become a groupie!

➤ OPTION #5: *Pretend You're a Roadie*

Throw on some ripped jeans and a T-shirt, pick up some equipment and start carrying it around. If someone from the band crew asks who you are, just say you were hired by the college to help out. Trust us; they will put you to work; once inside, hide out until the concert starts. Hey, if you do a good job, maybe you can make a career out of it. Quit med school and travel around lifting shit and doing drugs.

➤ OPTION #6: *Join the Campus Entertainment Group*

They book bands, comics, and all other forms of entertainment. It's a great group to join, especially if you aspire to be a club promoter one day.

52. You Don't Know How to Chug Beer

You are hanging at a party. "See that guy with the Santa Claus hat and no pants surrounded by girls," you say to your friend. "That's who I want to be."

You've seen these guys at parties wherever you go. Guys who can chug beer so well that they always draw a crowd. "Chug, Chug, Chug!" the crowd enthusiastically cheers them on. Man, if only you could chug beer like that you'd be the coolest kid on campus.

The WTF Approach to Honing the F*#!-ing Chug

➤ OPTION #1: *Practice Makes Perfect*

First off, lose the straw. You can't use a straw to suck Bud Light out of a plastic cup. What the fuck are you thinking? Next, get a six-pack or two and sit in your room so you can concentrate. Get your roommate to hold your mouth open and pour away. Throw up as necessary.

➤ OPTION #2: *Don't Learn*

Bring champagne to all the parties you attend. Chicks will think you're sophisticated.

➤ OPTION #3: *Learn How to Smoke Weed*

At least learn to smoke weed if you can't chug beer. This is college after all—you should learn something.

WHAT TO MASTER AFTER THE ART OF BEER CHUGGING:

Wine and liquor chugging: This is a very easy transition to make—even for you, dumbass.

Sword swallowing: Perform this tricky skill on campus during lunch or at parties and you can earn a few extra bucks. Who knows, you could make a career out of it if you get good enough. In this shit economy, it's good to have a backup career when you're studying finance. You need something reliable and recession proof.

Deep throating: Make sure to chug a lot of beer first—it makes sucking dick a lot easier and more appealing. You could make a career out of it. Everyone needs a side-job nowadays.

53. You're Not Invited to Any of the Cool Parties

You thought that college would be different—a clean slate with new friends and new girls who don't know that you wet yourself in your ninth-grade history class. This was your chance to start over. Remake yourself. But it didn't take long to learn that just like in high school you aren't getting invited to the cool parties. In fact, the last party you went to was a Dungeons & Dragons get-together where you were asked to guard the chips in case any archers or unicorns came in to steal them.

The WTF Approach to Getting Around Not Getting a F*#!-ing Invite

➤ OPTION #1: *Crash It*

College parties are cluster-fucks, so just walk in behind a big group of people. If someone asks who you're with, say you were invited by some dude named Jeff. There's got to be a Jeff in there somewhere.

➤ OPTION #2: *Dress in Drag*

Chicks always get priority when it comes to getting into parties. True, it won't be as easy to meet girls dressed as a chick, but when else would you have a chance to have lesbian sex? And don't worry if you don't look very good as a girl, just make a few hot girlfriends and go with them—there's always one ugly chick with a group of hotties.

➤ OPTION #3: *Work at a Bar*

Even if you are not twenty-one yet, most bars in most states allow you to work in bars at eighteen. Become a bar-back, doorman, waiter, whatever, just get in and make sure it's a cool joint. Working at a local bar can turn a loser like you into everyone's best friend.

➤ OPTION # 4: *Get Revenge*

If you still can't manage to sneak into the cool parties, then ruin the fun for everyone else. Call the cops and give those "cool" kids a night they'll never forget.

POP QUIZ

Choose the cool party.
- **A.** Hey, I'm having a couple of really nice people over for good conversation.
- **B.** Um, what are you up to tonight? Wanna, like, come over or whatever?
- **C.** A group of us are getting together to watch the *Dancing with the Stars* finale. You in, bro?
- **D.** Want to get totally fucked up?

Answer: D, jackass, D!

COLLEGE KID QUOTE

" I worked at one of the local bars at school for about three months. Turns out, that's all it took to get me laid a lot. "

—Steven Stanler, sophomore at the University of Alabama

54. You Throw a Party and No One Comes

You have been planning it for over a week. Facebook invites have gone out. Texts and e-mails have been sent. You got the keg and are ready to go. At first you just think everyone is fashionably late. They'll be here, you say; they're just at another party first. But when it's gets to be 1 A.M., it's quite clear that no one is coming to your party.

The WTF Approach to Dealing with a Failed F*#!-ing Party

> **STEP #1: *Cry***

Yes, a good cry is always helpful. Now continue to Step #2.

> **STEP #2: *Get Drunk and Pass Out***

Drink everything you have until your body shuts down. There's a good chance you'll black out and forget everything, so when you wake up you'll think that you must have thrown a real rager. Or you'll overdose and die, and therefore you won't care, and everyone will immortalize you.

> **STEP #3: *Lie***

Tell everyone they missed the party of a lifetime. Download some pictures of other parties from another school and post them on your Facebook page.

When someone asks you who came, just tell them there were too many people to keep track. In fact, you think there were people from another college there, then tell them you blacked out and don't remember the rest of the night.

PROFESSOR TIP: Next time, throw a theme party. People love that cheesy shit. Any excuse to dress like an ass and get wasted.

GREAT THEME PARTY IDEAS:

- '80s party
- Toga party
- Cross-dressing party
- Famous dead celebrities
- Virgins and hos

NOT SO GREAT THEME PARTY IDEAS:

- AA meeting
- Famous serial killers
- 9/11

IN THE FUTURE . . .

Get some friends, asshole!

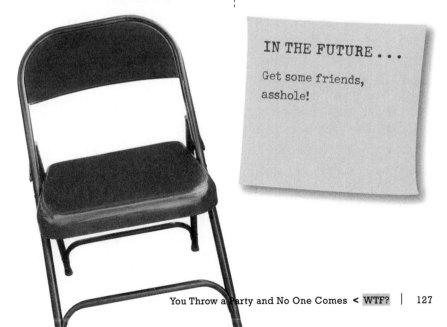

55. You Realize That College Life Has Made You a Drunk

A breakfast of tequila body-shots done off your roommate's fat beer belly is not the normal way to spend the hour before your morning class. Neither is having a three-martini lunch while everyone else is at Taco Bell. Nor is filling up a Big Gulp with Sprite and vodka and bringing it to class . . . actually, that's pretty normal for college come to think of it. But you get the idea: You are drinking way too much and if you don't stop, your liver is going to be on display in biology class—not in twenty or thirty years, but by next semester.

The WTF Approach to Getting Off the F*#!-ing Bottle

➤ STEP #1: *Limit Yourself*

Try to slow it down a bit and not drink like an idiot. When this inevitably fails, go to #2.

➤ STEP #2: *Get a Girlfriend*

After all, most of the time, you are drinking to get laid. Also, girlfriends have a way of creating stability—boredom, yes, but stability as well. Substitute Friday nights binge-drinking with your boys with Netflix with your lady.

Get some popcorn, put on a chick flick, and cuddle under the blankets. We admit you'll probably have to medicate somehow to make this tolerable. A Xanax or two should suffice. Make sure to use this boring downtime with a girlfriend to study more, work out, and get off booze. When you finally get sober and healthy, dump her ass, call your old buddies, and hit the bars. You'll look better so you should be able to score chicks without drinking—and getting them to drink—so much.

➤ STEP #3: *Join AA*

If getting a girlfriend didn't solve the problem, then get some professional help. We at *WTF* encourage that. However, just promise us that you won't turn into a born-again Christian just to stay on the wagon. Jesus didn't make you quit, you did. FYI: Jesus turned water into wine, not the other way around.

Weed—the Other Addictive Treat

Boozing isn't the only bad habit you
might pick up on campus. Chances
are you'll toke up in the dorms as well.
Here's a checklist to keep handy in
case you constantly find yourself with
the munchies.

YOU MIGHT BE A POTHEAD IF . . .

❑ You have a lifetime subscription to *High Times*.
❑ You *really* think that the Grateful Dead was a great band.
❑ At the end of watching a good movie, you always say that it would
   be better if you were stoned.
❑ You refuse to eat brownies unless they're smothered with THC.
❑ You wear Birkenstocks.

POP QUIZ

Match the drug with the corresponding major
of the drug user.

1.	Pot	A.	Sports Medicine
2.	Alcohol	B.	Music
3.	Heroin	C.	Native American Studies
4.	Acid	D.	Art
5.	Meth	E.	Chemistry
6.	Steroids	F.	Creative Writing
7.	Peyote	G.	Don't remember

Answers: 1G, 2F, 3B, 4D, 5E, 6A, 7C

56. You Run Out of Booze at a Party

The party is going great. Everyone is having a blast. The girl you have been hitting on all night is almost drunk enough for you to bang; all she needs is that last drink to get her wasted enough to find you attractive. You rush over to the keg . . . empty. You run over to the table with the hard stuff . . . gone. People are starting to leave when they realize there is no more booze, and your slutty conquest is about to bail.

The WTF Approach to Fixing a F*#!-ing Dry Party

> **OPTION #1: Go Buy More**

Do you really need a handbook to figure this out, dipshit?

> **OPTION #2: Party Like a Rock Star**

If all the stores are closed, then you're going to have to get creative. When Mötley Crüe ran out of heroin one night, these rock and rollers famously mainlined Jack Daniels instead. Collect all the booze and beer bottles you can and pour whatever is left in them into a big jug. Then, get some needles (if you don't have any, then you don't know how to party anyway—there's got to be one junkie among you), and take turns shooting the alcoholic mixture into your veins. If you don't get drunk, at least you can say that you did it. If you survive, that is.

NOTE: Before attempting, look at Mötley Crüe now.

> **OPTION #3: *Drink Listerine***

Listerine has 35 percent alcohol—that's 70 proof! (Most whiskeys are about 80 proof.) Vanilla extract and cough syrup also make for delicious cocktail mixers.

NOTE: Before attempting, watch an episode of *Intervention.*

WHAT THE F*#! IS UP WITH . . . ROBO-TRIPPIN'

The undisputed "king" of household, over-the-counter drugs that can really spice your party up is Robitussin. Robitussin contains a high concentration of dextromethorphan, a chemical that gets you really fucked up. Robitussin is such a popular choice for teenagers looking to get high that the slang term *robo-trippin'* has entered into the vernacular of morons around the country.

WOMAN GETS DUI FOR CLEAN BREATH

After a wild night of three glasses of Listerine, Carol Ries, 50, of Adrian, Michigan, rear-ended a vehicle. She pleaded guilty to drunk driving and will serve two years' probation. She blew a .30. on her BAC test; Michigan's legal limit is .08.

On a related charge, she plead not guilty to gingivitis.

> **OPTION #4: *Get High—Somehow***

Not only is your house a veritable cocktail bar once you know how to find that hidden alcohol, but it's also a veritable pharmacy as well. You'd be surprised how many common household items can be party savers. You can do "whip-its" with whip cream, or sniff things like glue or magic markers.

NOTE: Before attempting, . . . *really?*

> **OPTION #5: *Rock Out with Your Cocks Out***

Who needs liquor and drugs? Have everyone strip down and rock out with their cocks out. Do it, bro!

57. Your Trip Goes Bad During the Homecoming Parade

Mushrooms are completely natural, and they last for hours. So when your friend offered you some you thought it would be a good idea. But what wasn't a good idea was to take more than you could handle during the homecoming parade. Now you are tripping balls in a crowd of thousands!

The WTF Approach to Surviving a F*#!-ing Bad Trip

➤ OPTION #1: *Join the Parade*

Get in back of the marching band and move to your own groove. Everyone will think you are part of the interpretive dance group.

➤ OPTION #2: *Hide Out*

The last thing you want is to be in a large mass of people, especially when your magical ride takes a turn for the worse. Head back to your dorm or apartment ASAP, but don't go alone. You should have at least one other person around you, preferably someone who also took the mushrooms and is a veteran.

IN THE FUTURE . . .

Plan your drug use to coincide with trip-appropriate events.

► OPTION #3: *Man Up*

Conquer your fears, and deal with your haunted past. Tell the 'shrooms who's boss and turn your bad trip into a good one.

WTFACT: Psilocybin mushrooms (also called psilocybian mushrooms or teónanácatl) are fungi mainly of the *Psilocybe* genus that contain the psychedelic substances psilocybin and psilocin, and occasionally other psychoactive tryptamines. They also grow on cow, horse, pig, sheep, or even goat shit. Happy eating!

THINGS TO AVOID WHILE TRIPPING:

- Ex-girlfriend that you cheated on
- Thanksgiving dinner with the family
- Finals
- A root canal
- Hunting
- Gym class
- Walking a tightrope
- Car crash

THINGS TO DO WHILE TRIPPING:

- Finger paint
- Compose music
- Walk on the beach
- Hike up a mountain on a star-sprinkled night
- Group sex after hiking up a mountain on a star-sprinkled night
- Drive through a car wash
- Go to the planetarium
- Watch Pink Floyd's *The Wall*, or an actual wall—equally entertaining

POP QUIZ

Match the drug to the event.

1.	Ecstasy	A.	Pink Floyd Concert
2.	Weed	B.	Cleaning the Garage
3.	Meth	C.	Rave
4.	Cocaine	D.	Anytime
5.	'Shrooms	E.	Strip Club

Answers: 1C, 2D, 3B, 4E, 5A

58. The Cops Show Up at Your Party

Ah, the college party. There's nothing like it. You'll never forget the endless supply of weed, the fascinating beer chugging contests, or the line of hot wasted chicks waiting to vomit in the bathroom. Yes, there ain't no party like a college party. That is, until the cops show up.

The WTF Approach to Dealing with the F*#!-ing Five-Oh

➤ STEP #1: *Shut Everyone Up*

Quieting down a party won't be easy, but if you can do it successfully you might be able to save the night. The reason the cops left the doughnut shop to come there in the first place is because of the noise. So shut up and party on!

➤ STEP #2: *Stash the Evidence*

Drugs, underage girls, underage boys, goats in lingerie—hide all the illegal party

favors in the closet in case the boys in blue do come in.

➤ STEP #3: *Remember the Alamo*

If the cops do come in, follow the Beastie Boys' lead and "Fight for Your Right (to Party!)"—go for it. You might die or end up in jail for the rest of your life, but that would be so bugged out and trippy it would be worth it, right? Totally.

What Not to Do

Offer them a drink. Don't try to make friendly with the cops and offer them a beer or a hit of weed. Cops are cops because either their dad was a cop or because they are miserable people looking to punish anyone having a good time.

IN THE FUTURE . . .

Instead of alcohol being the drug of choice, give your guests opium. Sure, it's dangerous, but at least it will mellow everyone out. You'll have the quietest (yet most fun) party on campus.

Chapter 6

Extracurriculars

WTF?

59. You Need to Build Your Resume but You Hate People

You have never really liked others—and they never really liked you. With the exception of a few close buddies, you're a loner and you prefer it that way. But unfortunately, employers and graduate schools have this crazy idea that it is important to be able to work well with others. So it's time to bite the bullet and sign up for some social activities—even though inside you hate everyone.

The WTF Approach to Picking a F*#!-ing Activity

> **OPTION #1: *Join the Suicide Prevention Hotline***

Misery loves company. You'll get to volunteer to talk to miserable fucks all day. And since you hate people anyway, you'll probably get a kick out of it.

> **OPTION #2: *Join the Chess Club***

These nerds are also socially challenged loners. They sit in silence for hours devising strategies to destroy their opponents, but the minute anyone fucks with them in real life they bow down like the cowardly dogs that they are. This club would be perfect for you. Not only is there very little social interaction, but you can also bully anyone who does try to talk to you. Watch out for the one Russian kid who might be tougher than you think.

➤ OPTION #3: *Work with Animals*

Join a group that rescues animals or finds stray puppies loving homes. Hopefully you can spend most of your time with the animals rather than other human beings.

➤ OPTION #4: *Lie*

Put whatever you want on your resume. Employers don't even call and check on your last job, let alone what friggin' clubs you belonged to. This is your first lesson about real life. Just don't go overboard and say you were the president of the Spanish club when all you know in Spanish is *hola* and *Taco Bell*.

CLUBS *NOT* ACCEPTED BY THE STUDENT GOVERNMENT BOARD:

- Waterboarding club
- 2 + 2 = 5 club
- Inquisition Reenactment club
- My Girlfriend Is a Whore club
- Professors We Want to Fuck club
- Kill Whitey club
- 9/11 Was NOT a Conspiracy club
- AIDS is Hip club

60. Your Editor Takes the Byline on Your Article

You were the one who discovered the story. You were the one to locate and interview the sources. You were the one to crack the case. And you were the one who wrote the damn thing. This was going to be your breakout story. Yes, when this baby prints you'll be a star. But then it happened. The morning the paper comes out, you flip to your article and see that your name is nowhere to be found. In fact, it's been replaced by your editor's. Is this really happening? You look again. And again. And again. Finally you realize that this is no hallucination—that prick editor stole your work. WTF?

The WTF Approach to Getting the Recognition You F*#!-ing Deserve

➤ STEP #1: *Confront Him*

Perhaps it was an editorial oversight. If he admits the mistake and promises to run a correction, let him go. If he smiles and tells you that he doesn't know what you are talking about, move to Step #2.

➤ STEP #2: *Make Him Confess*

Barge into his shitty little office, grab him by his collar, and throw him up against the wall. Tell him that you just want him to admit what he did—that he at least owes you that much. When he inevitably spills the beans, make sure that you get that bitch on tape. Then show him the tape recorder, laugh in his face, and threaten to play the tape on the school radio station unless he makes a formal statement stating that your name was accidentally removed from the byline and replaced with his. He might lose his job over the oversight, but it's better than being outed as a crook.

➤ STEP #3: *Torture Him*

If he is a surprisingly tough college newspaper editor, you have to get creative. Shoot him with a tranquilizer gun, tie him up, and

for the ladies . . .

You can always use your feminine wiles to get him to confess and run a correction about the byline. Then again, if you are writing for the school paper, you might not have a lot of feminine wiles to begin with.

then proceed to beat the shit out of him when he wakes up until he talks. Then write a controversial article about the effectiveness of torture in certain situations. You might go to jail, but at least you'll finally see your name in print.

61. You Lose Your Voice Right Before the Big Debate

This is it. As captain, it's the debate you've been waiting for. You've perfected your arguments on the state of education in the United States, on American foreign policy in the twenty-first century, and why slavery was really not as bad as people make it out to be. But when you wake up the morning of the big debate you realize you have lost your voice.

The WTF Approach to Coming Through on the Big F*#!-ing Day

➤ OPTION #1: *Drink Up*

Yes, drinking tea is totally gay unless you're from England, but it does work. You could also try hitting the hard stuff. Certain liquors will soothe the throat. Blackberry brandy and Grand Marnier are alternatives to sipping on tea. Careful though, you don't want to overdo it and vomit on your opponent.

➤ OPTION #2: *Get a Voice Box*

Stephen Hawking has used one for over twenty years and look how brilliant he is. Chair-bound, but brilliant.

➤ OPTION #3: *Learn Sign Language—Fast*

Hey, it's a great language to learn. Think about all of the deaf conversations you will be able to eavesdrop on. Make sure you bring a translator along—or else it will just look like a bad game of charades.

Great Ad Hominem Arguments

They teach you on the debate team that *argumentum ad hominem* (Latin for "arguments against the man") are not effective, and that you should attack your opponent's positions and the logic of his arguments, rather than attack him personally. But we know that in the real world this is bullshit, and sometimes a personal jab is more effective than picking apart the most flawless of arguments. Here is a list of great ad hominem arguments we suggest you use if the debate isn't going your way:

- At least I don't wear women's panties.
- I fucked your girlfriend.
- I fucked your mom.
- I bet you have AIDS.
- You smell.

GREAT AD HOMINEM COMEBACKS

Here are some classic comebacks you can employ if someone else makes an ad hominem attack on *you*:

I know you are, but what am I?

I'm rubber and you're glue, whatever you say bounces off me and sticks to you.

Talk to the hand (extend your arm and show the palm of your hand next to the opponent's face)

Is someone talking? There is some dumb noise in here (pretend not to hear them).

You smell.

IN THE FUTURE . . .

Take care of yourself. Lay off the cigarettes and try not to get sick. And don't go down on that girl with the cold!

62. Your Knee Gives Out and You Lose Your Wrestling Scholarship

You were born to wrestle. Gifted with speed and strength, you were a natural from the start. And you loved it. After all, who doesn't get off on grabbing another sweaty man tightly from behind and violently pinning him down on a mat? Your hard work and genetic predisposition for whipping ass paid off big time when it earned you a scholarship to an Ivy League school—it certainly wasn't your essay in which you painfully attempted to use wrestling as a metaphor for life. But just when things are going great, your knee gives out and with it your scholarship, your future, and your reason for living. Now what?

The WTF Approach to Getting Back on Your F*#!-ing Feet

➤ OPTION #1: *Make a Miraculous Recovery*

Prove your teammates, your coach, and all the doctors wrong and make a recovery no one could have predicted. Make sure to write about your experiences so you can sell it as some shitty television movie of the week. Think *Lifetime*.

►OPTION #2: *Get a Lawyer*

The terms of your scholarship might need scrutiny from a legal eye. If it does say that you are screwed in the event of an injury, sue anyway. You can sue for anything in this country, and now that you're a crippled jack-ass with no way to finance your education you don't have many other options.

►OPTION #3: *Do Gay Porn*

Come on, you know you like dudes or you wouldn't have picked this sport. You think it's a coincidence that wrestling was passed down from the ancient Greeks, who spent all their free time philosophizing, sucking dick, and philosophizing about sucking dick? Seriously, and you're used to being on all fours anyhow. Just think of it as wres-tling without the tights—and with a cock in your ass.

WHAT THE F*#! IS UP WITH . . .
OLYMPIC SPORTS

Every four years Americans go gaga over athletes who are good at crap that no one cares about—like wrestling or swimming. Consider the hype over Michael Phelps. When was the last time you watched a swimming contest at your local sports bar? Four years ago when some shaved freak was squirming his way toward another gold medal, that's when.

The time has come for us to be honest about these so called "sports." Who gives a shit about fencing except for the French? And what about the shotput? When was the last time a kid in grade school wanted to be the world's best archer?

So, new rules for the Olympics: The more competitive, the more weight the award carries. Events can be broken down into gold, silver, and bronze events—just like the winning positions are now. But there will only be one winner for each event—no more three winners. After all, the only thing less impressive than being the world's best discus thrower is to be the second- or third-best discus thrower.

So let's stick to real sports that we like and are good at. Sports like baseball, basketball, volleyball, and tennis (as long as one of those hot sisters is playing or John McEn-roe comes out of retirement). Game over.

63. You Run for Student Government to Impress a Girl but Are Deathly Afraid of Public Speaking

You have been following the girl of your dreams around campus for months now. You even tried getting into the classes she is taking just so you could get to know her. It seemed hopeless, but now at last you see your chance. She is involved in student government and re-elections are coming up. Before you know it, you are signing on the dotted line to participate in the pre-election speeches and debate. You are now officially running for office, even though you are deathly afraid of speaking in public.

The WTF Approach to Making a F*#!-ing Speech

➤ STEP #1: *Hypnosis*

This is actually a good place to start if you really plan on taking the stage without pissing yourself.

Hypnotherapy has helped many people overcome their fears. You might even find out what started your fear of public speaking.

➤ STEP #2: *Imagine Them in Their Underwear*

Yes, this is an oldie but a goodie. Imagining people in a less intimidating way can help calm your nerves. Heads up though, you don't want to look at a hot girl in the crowd and imagine her in a pink thong. It's very difficult to debate anything with a raging hard-on.

➤ STEP #3: *Grow Some Balls*

Conquer your fears. Get up there, make your speech, and debate those other pricks. And while you're at it, use your closing argument as an opportunity to ask that girl out.

WTFACT: Speaking in public is the number one fear among people. Death is number two. (Hooking up with a tranny is number four.)

Worst Malapropisms in Public Speaking

Out of all the stupid things ever uttered on record, former vice president Dan Quayle can proudly say that he is the speaker of many of them. He's hands-down the worst speaker in human history. Here are some of his famous malapropisms.

- "Republicans understand the importance of bondage between a mother and child."
- "One word sums up probably the responsibility of any vice president, and that one word is 'to be prepared.'"
- "I believe we are on an irreversible trend toward more freedom and democracy—but that could change."
- "I love California, I practically grew up in Phoenix."
- "I stand by all the misstatements that I've made."

64. You Get Dropped from the Campus Improv Group

You love Second City, The Groundlings, and Upright Citizens Brigade. You never missed an episode of *Whose Line is it Anyway?* So when you joined your school's improv troupe you felt like you were on your way to becoming the next Wayne Brady, or at least on your way to getting some hot ass. Girls love comics, right? But just before the big show, you get the news: You're out of the group. Now it's official—you're not funny and you're a loser.

The WTF Approach to Recovering from a F*#!-ing Ejection

➤ OPTION #1: *Ignore It*

Shit, it's just improv. Keep showing up at the shows and start improving your way into the scenes. What are they going to do, stop the show? The audience will think this is all part of the performance. Who knows, the other improvisers might get so pissed they start a fight. Then it will really be a good show.

➤ OPTION #2: *Start Your Own Group*

Most famous improv companies started because members of other groups wanted to go out on their own. Find a hot spot and start your own group. Make sure to cast hot, big-breasted girls who like to do lesbian scenes. Trust me, nobody will ever go see your rival group perform again!

➤ OPTION #3: *Eat Their Pet Dogs*

Follow your former cast mates home and find out which ones have dogs. Capture the dogs, kill them, and eat them. Then send them a card that reads, *Sorry about your pet, but it's a dog-eat-dog world out there*. If this doesn't teach them what a tough business this is, nothing will.

➤ OPTION #4: *Embrace It*

Think of all the comics who have been kicked out of their groups and went on to fame. Norm McDonald got fired from *SNL* and look where he is now. On second thought, you should probably kill yourself.

The Basic Rules of Improv

Here are some guidelines to follow:

Rule #1: Don't deny it.

WTF: You're a douche bag.
Improviser: Yes I am.

Rule #2: Always say: "Yes, and . . ."

WTF: You're a douche bag.
Improviser: Yes, and I fucked your mom.

Rule #3: Raise the stakes.

WTF: You fucked my mom?
Improviser: Yes I did, and I also fucked your dad.

Rule #4: Add history.

WTF: I can't believe you fucked my mom and dad.
Improviser: And they said I was much better than you.

Rule #5: Play the opposite emotion.

WTF: They really said that?
Improviser: While we fucked.
WTF: That is . . . *awesome.* You must really be good in bed.

65. You Lose Your Government Seat to a Marxist

Commies. Reds. Pinkos. They're everywhere you look on campus. Hell bent on destroying the free market and the free world, these "social democrats" won't stop until every Wal-Mart is destroyed and replaced by a farmer's market filled only with locally grown organic fruit—or something like that anyway.

The WTF Approach to Winning Your F*#!-ing Seat Back

➤ STEP #1: *Run as a Fascist*

Fascism beat out communism in Germany, Italy, and Spain among other countries for a reason. According to the historian and political philosopher Hannah Arendt, fascism has a deeper, more powerful appeal because it plays upon our ancient ideas of tribe, nation, and race. In a nutshell, the statement "Workers of the world, unite" is not as powerful or appealing as "Let's conquer Poland and kill Jews."

If you have to, purge the whole campus of these raving lunatics and restore order with a temporary dictatorship that will in turn become a permanent dictatorship—but *with* Wal-Marts.

➤ STEP #2: *Run as a Hard-core Neoconservative*

Oh wait. Sorry, we just said this, right?

➤ STEP #3: *Send Her to the Gulags*

Teach this leftist nut about the real communism, Stalin style. Kidnap her and send her to Siberia and force her to do hard labor. Then we'll find out how she can help the prison camp according to her abilities, according to the camp's needs.

WHAT THE F*#! IS UP WITH . . . COMPARING EVERYONE TO NAZIS

The Republicans do it; the Democrats do it; *everyone* does it. Whenever a political pundit or a politician wants to make a point, they compare their opponent to a Nazi or a Nazi appeaser. This is absurd. Nobody was like the Nazis—except for the friggin' Nazis. That's why they were such unbelievable pricks.

Victory Is Yours

Sorry, but that's the only way to win. Once you get elected, however, you can do what you like. You don't really have to conquer Poland or kill Jews and, quite frankly, *WTF* implores you do resist the temptation, however great.

WHAT THE F*#! DID HE SAY?

"Communism is like one big phone company."—Lenny Bruce

"Communism is not love. Communism is a hammer which we use to crush the enemy."—Mao Tse-Tung

"When we hang the capitalists they will sell us the rope we use."—Joseph Stalin

"Democracy is the road to socialism."—Karl Marx

"If Karl had spent more time making capital than writing about it, he'd have been better off."—Karl Marx's Mother

---

66. You're the Only Gay Guy on the Football Team

You've known that you were gay since you were in junior high—gym class specifically. When you wrestled, you held on a little too long after the whistle blew. When you showered, you used a cranberry body wash instead of soap. And when you climbed the rope, you came. Now that you are in college word has gotten around that you're gay. It would have been one thing if you played football at San Francisco State, but your football scholarship led you to the University of Mississippi. Here's how to survive your time as a flaming Ole Miss Rebel.

The WTF Approach to Being the F*#!-ing Team Homo

➤ **OPTION #1: *Say You're Only into Asian Guys***

This should put your teammates' minds at ease since there are probably no Asian players on the team. There might be one big fat Samoan dude, but just tell him that you're not into "big fat Samoan dudes." After all, who the fuck would be?

➤ **OPTION #2: *Introduce Your Teammates to Girls***

As a natural consequence of your gayness, you're surely best friends with all the cheerleaders. Get your teammates laid and they'll forgive you for your sins. But one question remains: Will God?

➤ OPTION# 3: *Deny It*

No reason to let your team know what extracurricular activities you're interested in. Deny rumors that you're gay. If they wonder why you never have a girlfriend, tell them that you're very religious. If they find undeniable proof of your homosexual lifestyle and accuse you of lying, tell them your religion is like Christianity except it mandates that you suck cock.

➤ OPTION #4: *Pump Up*

Be the biggest dude on the team and those gay jokes will be a thing of the past. They'll be too scared you'll beat them up, pin them down, and go to town on their ass.

WTFACT: The North American Gay Amateur Athletic Alliance (NAGAAA) was created in 1977. NAGAAA's current membership includes over 680 teams from thirty-seven leagues throughout the United States and Canada.

➤ OPTION #5: *Wear two cups.*

To make the team feel secure, put on an extra jock strap and cup so that your penis is even farther away from their assholes.

TEAM NAMES *NOT* APPROVED BY THE NAGAAA:

- The San Francisco Giant Dicks
- The Toronto Blue Balls
- Milwaukee Spewers
- Arizona Barebacks
- Houston Assholes
- Pittsburgh Butt Pirates
- Tampa Bay Gays
- Oakland AIDS

IN THE FUTURE . . .

Choose to focus on more traditionally gay sports like gymnastics, fencing, and cockfighting.

67. Your A Capella Group Has a Concert and No One Shows Up

After countless hours rehearsing and getting each song down perfect, the night has arrived. Your a cappella group is warming up backstage waiting for the show to start. But the start time has come and gone, and shit, *no one* is in the audience.

The WTF Approach to Reacting to an Empty F*#!-ing Auditorium

➤ OPTION #1: *Start a Riot*

There's never really a good excuse to start a riot, but this is as good as any. Band together your fellow singing nerds and start trashing the campus. Make sure everyone knows this is what happens when you don't support the arts!

➤ OPTION #2: *Get a Life*

What are you doing in an a capella group anyway? This is a group for people who just sit around and sing without music. If you really want to sing so badly, drop out of the group, get some tattoos, start doing drugs, and join a band, loser.

➤ OPTION #3: *Sing*

The show must go on. Sure it will be depressing, but when your friends ask you how the show was you can tell them it was awesome.

Yeah, as if a nerd like you has friends.

➤ OPTION #4: *Fill the Seats*

Grab some homeless people off the streets. You can use some cheap liquor to bribe them to come in and watch the show. At least they'll be honest. If they don't like it even with the liquor, you know you suck.

➤ OPTION #5: *Take It on the Road*

Start an impromptu off-season caroling troupe and go dorm to dorm and force these assholes to listen to you. You did all that rehearsing and damn it, they're going to hear it whether they like it or not!

Singing Queens

If you belong to an a cappella group, you might be gay. Here are some of today's most successful a cappella groups . . . you be the judge.

FAMOUS GAY A CAPELLA GROUPS:

- Ball in the House
- The Blenders
- The Blanks
- Boyz Night out
- Cosmos

LESS FAMOUS GAY A CAPELLA GROUPS:

- The Cocks
- The Cock Lovers
- The Fat Cocks
- The Fat Cock Lovers
- The Gay Fat Cock Loving Gay Boys

IN THE FUTURE . . .

Book your group at gay bars. You'll be a hit in no time. They love that shit.

68. You Try Out for the Basketball Team and They Make You the Mascot

Jocks get all the hot chicks. This has been true for centuries, and probably won't ever change. You can bet that the gymnastics majors in ancient Greek schools were probably getting a lot more ass than philosophy students. True, it was probably little-boy ass, but that's not the point.

So you figured you'd try out for the basketball team in college, even though you sat on the bench for most of your high school basketball career. And surprise, you didn't make it. However, you were so awesomely bad that they asked you to become the mascot.

The WTF Approach to Getting Over Getting F*#!-ing Cut

➤ OPTION #1: *Go with It*

While you may look like a complete jerk-off dancing around in a big bird outfit, you'll be invited to all the team events and parties. If you play your cards right and act like the fuzzy little friendly creature you pretend to be, you might just be able to bag a hot pom-pom girl who recently broke up with the quarterback.

➤OPTION #2: *Hit the Gym*

Maybe you didn't make the cut because you just aren't pumped up enough. Start lifting heavy weights and bulk up for tryouts next year. Even if you don't make it on the team, at least you'll be so ripped that you can get laid anyway.

➤OPTION #3: *Kill the Team*

Think of the 1972 Olympic Games in Munich when Arab terrorists killed all those Israeli athletes. If you get away with it, you might just make second or third string.

***WTF*ACT:** "Knickerbocker" refers to the style of pants New York City's Dutch settlers wore, known as "knickerbockers," or "knickers."

Give Geronimo a Break

Look, if Native Americans object to the way in which they're portrayed in sports—like in the case of the Washington Redskins or the Cleveland Indians—then pick another name for your team. We stole their land, killed their buffalo, and gave them small pox. Let them bitch; they've earned it.

***WTF*ACT:** "Dodger" as in the Los Angeles Dodgers (formerly the Brooklyn Dodgers) refers to the many trolley cars that crisscrossed Brooklyn in the early twentieth century—so many in fact that Brooklynites literally had to "dodge" them.

Team Names Should Fit

The New York Knicks (Knicker-bockers), the San Francisco 49ers, the Houston Oilers—these team names reflect the history and the character of the place they represent. But other team names just don't.

Take the Utah Jazz. What the hell do Mormons know about jazz? New Orleans gave birth to jazz, not Salt Lake City. Seriously, you can't give a name like Jazz to one of the whitest and most conser-vative states in the union. What's next, the Wyoming Funk?

NOTE: Sports expert and retired U.S. Army lieutenant colonel Paul Munier (grandfather extraordinaire) pointed out in the edit-ing phase of this book that the Utah Jazz moved from New Orleans as an expansion team. This note may ruin the above joke, but it's better than disappointing The Colo-nel. Trust us.

Rejected College Sports Team Names

These college team names, for whatever reason, were rejected by the NCAA:

- University of Mississippi Segregationists
- University of West Virginia Dirty, Filthy Coal Miners
- University of California, Berkeley Commie Bastards
- University of Alaska Cold-ass Motherfuckers
- Borough of Manhattan Community College African-Americans, Puerto Ricans, and Gregory Bergman

WTF FOLLOW-UP READING

Mascots: Football's Furry Friends by Rick Minter

Chapter 7

Spring Break

69. You Can't Afford to Go on Spring Break

You have been looking forward to Spring Break ever since you got into college. Every time you watch a *Girls Gone Wild* video you imagine yourself right in the middle of a naughty coed's massive breasts. But you have only five bucks in your bank account and your parents refuse to give you any money for something that is not a learning experience (little do they know).

The WTF Approach to Being a F*#!-ing Broke Spring Breaker

➤ OPTION #1: *Sell Drugs*

This is the quickest way to make some good cash, as well as some good connections. Don't smoke your own stash—or the only place you'll be going to for Spring Break is rehab.

➤ OPTION #2: *Stay Home*

Tell your friends that you and a buddy from home are going to Amsterdam for Spring Break, then go home to Mom and Dad and catch up on your sleep. Photoshop some drunken pics of you in the red light district and brag about how awesome your trip was.

" My girlfriend went on Spring Break without me, so I decided to have sex with as many girls as I could. That's what I call a break. "

—Elliot Jameson, junior at the University of Massachusetts

➤ OPTION #3: *Mooch*

Borrow some cash from your friends for airfare and just wing the rest. Go to the bars and drink other people's drinks. Buy a loaf of bread for food, then crash on the floor in your friend's room. If you're resourceful, you can really get by on almost nothing and still have an awesome time.

for the ladies . . .

Please, when was the last time you paid for a fucking thing?

WTF ABOUT TOWN

We went to Cabo to check out the Spring Break scene:

WTF: Hey there.

Anna: Whoo-hoo party!

WTF: You're beautiful.

Anna: Thanks! Whoo-hoo party!

WTF: I thought you might want to be in the next *Girls Gone Wild* video.

Anna: OMG, are you like a producer?!

WTF: Sure, okay.

Anna: I totally want to be in that video! Whoo-hoo party!

WTF: Okay, do you have a problem taking off your top on camera?

Anna: Oh no, I hate my dad! Whoo-hoo party!

WTF: Action!

IN THE FUTURE . . .

Date rich girls. Girls love to take care of their guys. Let her pay for your trip. Then suggest Amsterdam.

70. You Get Kicked Out of Your Hotel Room

Turns out that hotel managers frown on running through the hotel halls singing "Happy Birthday" while wearing nothing but your birthday suit at 5 A.M. Go figure.

The WTF Approach to Finding Another F*#!-ing Place to Stay

➤ OPTION #1: *Hit the Motels*

Most places sell out quickly for Spring Break, but there just might be one or two rooms left. If not, you might have to offer Javier the hotel manager an extra fifty or a hand job to free up a room.

➤ OPTION #2: *Sleep on the Beach*

Hopefully you went somewhere warm with a beach. If not, you're a moron. Lay a blanket down and crash on the sand. You'll be so smashed anyway, you probably won't even know where you are. Just make sure you shower each morning, sand has a way of getting caught in your ass pipe.

➤ OPTION #3: *Get a Chick*

If you aren't bagging a chick every night on Spring Break then you're doing something wrong. If you can't seem to get the hot ones to take you home, go after a desperate-looking girl who's as horny and unlucky in love as you. Sure she might be a beast, but at least she's a beast with a bed. So get really wasted, then hit on her. When she takes you home, bang her good and you'll have a place to stay for the rest of the trip.

➤ OPTION #4: *Get Arrested*

Okay, it's not exactly how you wanted to spend your little vacation, but at least you'll have a place to stay and hopefully three squares a day. That's better than most of the natives in Cabo, so consider yourself lucky.

THE MOST OUTRAGEOUS PLACES TO CRASH:

- On a giant peach
- In the wardrobe to Narnia
- In a shoe with an old biatch
- Graceland
- Never, Neverland
- The Statue of Liberty
- In a whale

71. Your Girlfriend Goes to Cancun but You Have to Work

Spring Break is coming up and everyone is getting ready to go crazy. Sadly you just started an internship and can't skip out. What's worse, instead of staying behind with you, your girlfriend's been convinced by her slutty friends to go with them to Cancun. Cancun! Not to worry, though, she loves you and says she'll call every day. Like a fool you believe her. Then one night after work you turn on the TV only to see your girl on a live version of *Girls Gone Wild*!

The WTF Approach to Being Away from Your F*#!-ing Girl

➤ OPTION #1: *Quit*

Screw it, it's not a real job anyway, and a chick with those kind of real tits doesn't come around every day. Take the next flight and stop her before she ends up eating a skin burrito after a few Jäger bombs. If she gets pissed off at you for quitting your job to come to Cancun, dump her ass, and go have sex with a hot Mexican chick in front of her.

➤ OPTION #2: *Break Up with Her*

This will ensure she has a shitty time on Spring Break, and probably stop her from having sex with someone else—she'll be too busy texting you. Better to break her heart than contract herpes from the guy she banged on the beach. Then you can also feel free to have sex with some tramps while she's away. If she begs you to take her back when she returns, you should probably be the nice guy that you are and do it. Unless one of those tramps is really, really hot.

➤ OPTION #3: *Sell Her Off*

Contact a Mexican prostitution ring and act as her pimp. Tell them where she's staying and where they can wire the money. She wanted to experience the real Mexico, now she will.

WORST PLACES TO GO FOR SPRING BREAK:

- Your parents' house
- Utah
- Siberia
- Darfur
- Afghanistan (though we hear the opium is excellent!)

IN THE FUTURE . . .

Date a codependent girl who can't do anything without you.

72. You Drink the Water and Get the Runs

Spring Break in a foreign land like Mexico is all fun and games. That is, until you eat or drink something that turns your stomach into a perfect shit storm in the making. Yes, there is nothing worse than waiting in line at a crowded bar clenching your ass cheeks in a desperate hope to stave off a diarrhea diaspora that's about to add a permanent dash of color to your white swim trunks—and a permanent dent in your vacation.

The WTF Approach to Handling Montezuma's F*#!-ing Revenge

➤ OPTION # 1: *See a "Doctor"*

Everyone knows that other countries don't have *real* doctors—especially countries with a small Jewish population. But at least they're cheap. In fact, some really shitty countries will take your stool as payment.

➤ OPTION #2: *Embrace It*

Go back to the hotel and just deal with it. Compared to all your friends who will no doubt be sick from drinking, your little poo-poo problem might not be so bad.

***WTF*ACT:** It is estimated that 40 percent of foreign traveler vacations in Mexico are disrupted by infection. The other 60 percent? Kidnapping, mostly. Happy travels.

An Orgasmic Dump

Let's be honest. The only feeling that rivals an orgasm is taking a big dump when you really, really need to go. But why settle for experiencing each of these fabulous feelings separately? Why not cum and shit at the same time? Well, if you're interested in reaching the heights of euphoria, follow these steps:

1. Eat a lot Mexican or Indian food.
2. Watch your favorite porno the minute you finish eating.
3. Begin masturbating immediately while sitting on the toilet.

WHAT THE F*#! IS UP WITH . . .
BEING PROUD OF TAKING A SHIT

Don't pretend you've never at least once in your life looked down after a tremendous dump and been impressed by what you saw. "Wow, that came out of me?" you say, feeling a strange sensation of pride, as if you had done something special with your asshole. Pig.

◄ NOTE: If you are doing this with a partner then you are both filthy animals who do not deserve to live. There are some limits even for us. However, if you guys are set on doing the old "shit and screw," we suggest that you make love-and-poop in the bathtub.

73. You're Sleeping on the Beach and Your Friends Use Sunblock to Draw Phallic Shapes on You

Everyone knows when you drink in the sun you get drunk faster. You'll also get burned, and if you pass out around your drunk, immature friends, don't be surprised if you wake up with the tan lines of a giant dick on your face.

The WTF Approach to Dealing with F*#!-ing Dick Friends

➤ OPTION #1: *Self-Tanner*

Apply the lotion on the outline of the dick and blend it in with your current tan.

➤ OPTION #2: *Embrace It*

Make it your thing and have everyone call you Dick. Then act like one so people think you're cool.

for the ladies . . .

If this happens to you, just be thankful that it's just the tan lines of a dick and not a real dick on your face. Odds are if you pass out drunk in the sun on Spring Break that might actually happen!

➤ OPTION #3: *Play It Off*

Tell everyone it's a birthmark and play the sympathy card. Some chick with a good heart (and a love of cock) might take pity on you.

➤ OPTION #4: *Get Even*

They fucked with the wrong freshman. Drug them and carve "I love dick" into their chest and back using an ice pick. Not enough to kill them, but enough so that when they wake up they'll wish they were dead.

COLLEGE KID QUOTES

I woke up with a big schlong on my face. I mean, not a real one, like a drawing of one. No seriously, it wasn't like a real one.

—Anthony Depala, grad student at Princeton University

IN THE FUTURE . . .

Get tattoos all over, including your face. This way your friends won't be able to create inappropriate tan lines. Of course, you will look like a freaky piece of shit but at least you won't have a dick on your face.

74. You Get Arrested for No Good Reason

Spring Break has begun. The drinking, the girls, the sun. This is going to be a twenty-four-hour party, until you try to inconspicuously pull down your pants to take a piss and get arrested for indecent exposure and drunken misconduct. Now the only "happy hour" you know is the one hour a day you're not getting ass raped.

The WTF Approach to Beating Those F*#!-ing Foreign Charges

➤ OPTION #1: *Wait It Out*

Unless you have committed some serious crime, most college kids who are arrested during Spring Break get released within twenty-four to forty-eight hours.

➤ OPTION #2: *Flip the Switch*

Call a lawyer and tell the police that you plan on suing the shit out of them for sexual harassment, slander, and emotional damages. Then call *Jerry Springer* and tell them what "happy hour" means in Mexican prison.

➤ OPTION #3: *Break Out*

Take off all your clothes; tie them together to make a long rope. Then attach your belt to the end. Throw the homemade rope out and knock down the keys. Drag them to you and break out. Wait . . .

that was an episode of *The Brady Bunch*. Forget it, you're fucked!

➤OPTION #4: *Pay Off the Cops*

The good thing about corrupt countries that arrest you for nothing half the time is that you can get out for pennies. Throw them a few bucks and go home. Here's a rough estimate as to what it takes to get pardoned by *policía corrupta*:

- Drunk in public: $1
- Vandalism: $2
- Theft: $3
- Murder: $4—plus a $2 international processing fee if you kill an American

---

COLLEGE KID QUOTE

" The only day out of my Spring Break I remembered, was Spring Break court, because I was semi-sober there. "

—Jonathon Freeman, senior at University of Nevada

HOW YOU SPEND YOUR TIME ON SPRING BREAK

50%	drinking
10%	screwing
20%	bragging about all the chicks you scored
10%	vomiting and swearing never to drink again
10%	unaccounted time due to blackout

SPRING BREAK COURT

Did you know that many places have set up Spring Break courts? Yep, Spring Break court is where you have a quick trial and you carry out the sentence (usually community service) with a group of other Spring Breakers who committed a similar crime. This translates to cleaning the streets or the outside of the bars that kids partied in the night before. It sucks, but you are done quickly and usually don't have to pay a fine.

75. You Lose Your Passport and Can't Get Back in the Country

Well, Spring Break is over and after a week of nonstop boozing, smoking, and the occasional blackout, you're looking forward to getting home to rest. But just as you get to the airport, you realize that somewhere in your drunken travels you lost your passport. WTF?

The WTF Approach to Breaking Back into the F*#!-ing Country

➤ STEP #1: *Call Your Parents*

Have them come and get you. They should have your birth certificate and other proof of your citizenship. If they don't have your birth certificate, then they don't love you or you were adopted, in which case you don't want to go home anyway.

➤ STEP #2: *Live in the Airport*

If it's good enough for Tom Hanks, it's good enough for you. You have everything you need in an airport. Plus, you can bang hot chicks and you'll never have to see them again. That beats college.

It looks like this is your new home for now, so you better learn to communicate with the locals. Get a job and a place to stay. Maybe one day you'll see your family and friends again.

➤STEP #4: *Cross Illegally*

When you've finally tired of tequila and dysentery, do what thousands of Mexicans do all the time. Hire a coyote—a guide that will take you over the river and through the desert—and head to the Promised Land. Then get a job bussing tables or picking strawberries until you save up enough money to get the rest of the way home.

Nontraditional Spring Break Destinations

For those of you who are sick of Daytona Beach and Cancun, there are other more exotic places to go for Spring Break.

Here are the top five worldwide destinations:

1. **Thailand.** Want to have more sex in the sun than you could possibly imagine? Bangkok makes Cancun look like New Hampshire—in the winter. Why do you think they call it Bangkok? Because that's all they know how to do.
2. **Rio.** Ever seen that *City of God* movie? Doesn't that look fun?
3. **Australia.** Sun, surf, blondes. It's like California but with fucked-up English-type accents.
4. **Tokyo.** These little people like to party big. Enjoy some sake and some sucky at the same time!
5. **Amsterdam.** Legal prostitution. Legal marijuana. Little cute Jewish girls who like to keep diaries while hiding from Nazis. What more could you want?

Chapter 8

Going Greek

76. You Go to Rush Week but No Fraternity Wants You

Fraternities are about brotherly love. One for all and all for one. Think of the Three Musketeers but with beer bongs, a ton of weed, and pizza for breakfast, lunch, and dinner—every day. But no matter what you do, you just can't seem to get into one. You've interviewed and interviewed, but no frat seems to want you.

The WTF Approach to Becoming a Popular F*#!-ing Pledge

> **OPTION #1: *Learn to Chug Beer***

If you can't already chug beer like a pro, learn (see page 122). Develop a reputation for being the best beer chugger in school and every moronic fraternity will be looking for *you*.

> **OPTION #2: *Offer a Bribe***

Offer them money and maybe they'll let your stupid ass in. You'll be surprised how far a free month's supply of Dominos pizza can go.

> **OPTION #3: *Join a Sorority***

You wish, pervert.

FRATERNITY INTERVIEW TIPS:

- Change your name to Brad, Chad, or any other stupid white-bread name.
- Wear a shirt with a polo player, alligator, or douchebag stitched onto it.
- Use words and phrases like "right on," "bro," and "no doubt."
- Call every guy "boss" or "chief."
- Tell a fascinating anecdote, like the first time you almost died from drinking.

WTFACTS: More than you ever wanted to know about fraternities:

- Fraternity members acquire grade point averages above all other college men's scholastic rankings.
- Frat members have an overall higher graduation rate than non-Greeks.
- All but two U.S. presidents since 1825 were members of fraternities.
- Studies show that 76 percent of Congress, 71 percent of the men listed in *Who's Who in America,* and 85 percent of the *Fortune* 500 executives belong to a fraternity.
- Since 1910, 85 percent of the Supreme Court justices were first frat boys.

GREEK CELEBS

Some of the more recognizable celebrities who went the brotherhood route . . .

Steven Spielberg
Theta Chi

Bob Dole
Kappa Sigma

David Letterman
Sigma Chi

Ronald Reagan
Tau Kappa Epsilon

Woody Harrelson
Sigma Chi

Brad Pitt
Sigma Chi

Andrew Greenstein
Lambda Sigma Upsilon

Johnny Carson
Phi Gamma Delta

Greek Versus Greek

Sometimes it's hard to tell when people are using "Greek" to refer to fraternities and their members or actual Greek people. Here are some notable differences:

GREEKS FROM GREECE	GREEKS FROM FRATS
Used to be good at philosophy	Philosophy of life not fully worked out but definitely has something to do with pussy
Used to believe that the highest form of love was a sexually intimate relationship between an older teacher and his younger, male pupil	WTF? No fucking way, bro!
Used to believe that women were only good for sex and making babies	Feel the same way but don't want kids right now
Built the Parthenon	Always get the Parthenon and the Pantheon mixed up
Created the Olympics	Love to chant: USA! USA! USA! while chugging beer
Speak Greek	Know hookers who speak it.
Revere the ancient epic poet Homer	Revere TV cartoon character of the same name

77. Your Dad Wants You to Pledge His Frat but It's Full of Losers

You have been wearing Kappa Phi T-shirts and sweatshirts ever since you were a little kid. Your father has recounted his glory days as a Kappa Phi countless times, and ever since you can remember you were expected to be a Kappa Phi too. One problem, the Kappa Phi chapter at your school is a bunch of nerds. Dungeons & Dragons-playing, Trekkie-loving, computer-center nerds, and if you ever want to get a date in college you can't pledge this fraternity.

The WTF Approach to Pledging a F*#!-ing Nerd Frat

►OPTION #1: *Tell Dad the Truth*

Just explain that you love him and you're sure his Kappa Phi was amazing and there is no way your experience could ever live up to his if you pledge this chapter. If he still doesn't get it, invite him up for the weekend to introduce him to the fraternity at your school.

When he sees that the all-night toga parties are now late-night discussions of Aristotle, he'll understand.

►OPTION #2: *Pimp Your Frat*

Do an Extreme Makeover: Fraternity Edition. Once you're a brother, start changing the image of this fraternity for the better. They can still have their Dungeons & Dragons nights, just add a couple kegs, a stripper, and you got a party.

PROFESSOR TIP: Rent *Revenge of the Nerds*.

➤ **OPTION #3: *Transfer to Another School***

If your father is dead set on you becoming a Kappa Phi, this might be your only option.

Most Exclusive Fraternities

These are great fraternities but very difficult to get into:

Kappa Big Cocks: must be nine inches or more to pledge . . . very popular at Howard University

Theta Eskimos: have to be able to field dress a polar bear

Delta Pulitzer Prize Winners: if you can't write, forget it!

Phi Gamma Giants: under seven foot need not apply

PROS AND CONS OF GOING GREEK

Pros	Cons
Meet lots of people	Hazing
Parties	Being part of a herd
Working with others for a common goal	Pledging is a huge time commitment
Parties	Living with a bunch of dudes

78. Your Frat Strands You in the Middle of Nowhere

It's common knowledge that fraternities haze their pledges. One little prank they like to pull is to leave the pledges in the middle of nowhere without any money or a phone. Hysterical, right?

The WTF Approach to Finding Your F*#!-ing Way

➤ OPTION #1: *Man Up*

Start walking. Forrest Gump ran across the whole country, and he was an idiot. So you can make it a few miles. Use this time by yourself to think about all the fun you'll have when you get to torture the next batch of pledges.

➤ OPTION #2: *Hitch a Ride*

You have two thumbs—use them. People used to hitchhike across the country all the time. But be careful about accepting rides from long-haul truckers. They just love dem fresh young boys.

➤ OPTION #3: *Fake Your Own Death*

Turn your back on school, your friends, your family and start over with a new identity—and no student loans.

Things to Do in the Middle of Nowhere

History shows us that being lost has led to some of the greatest discoveries.

America: Christopher Columbus thought he was going to India, but he ended up somewhere next to Puerto Rico. Yes, we know that the so-called intellectual college professors tell you that the Vikings under Erik the Red discovered America, but there is no Erik the Red Day, so explain that. And, we know there were some people living here to begin with, but most of the time they were just messing around and preparing the turkey for Columbus and his Pilgrims.

The Dead Sea Scrolls: In 1947, some little Bedouin kid was looking for a goat—or something to screw—when he came across some old papers that he thought were toilet paper. Luckily he was taught to use his left hand to wipe his ass so he kept them clean. Thank God.

Atlantis: Just kidding, moron.

IN THE FUTURE . . .

Have a GPS chip implanted under your scrotum and get a friend to pick you up.

79. You Get Caught Stealing from a Rival Fraternity

It's a common tradition that while pledging, one of your required tasks is to steal something of value from another fraternity, like a television set, a Sony PlayStation, or in the case of the Ivy League, a relic from the Ming dynasty. Now, it's your turn to show what you're made of. You and the other pledges make it in and grab something, but just as you're about to get away, one of the frat brothers comes downstairs and catches *you* red-handed. Your pledge "brothers" have bolted.

The WTF Approach to Getting F*#!-ing Away with It

> **OPTION #1: *Act Insane***

Seriously, act like you are fucking out of your mind. Start mumbling about cheese and rainbows. Then ask if this is the land of Narnia and say that the king told you to get a treasure from Narnia and you were only obeying orders. Hopefully the other fraternity brothers will take pity on you and let you go.

> **OPTION #2: *Switch Teams***

Tell them you will become their spy and tell them everything that goes on in your fraternity if they let you go. They'll probably just kick the shit out of you, but it's worth a shot.

➤ OPTION #3: *Kick Them in the Nuts*

Lie down on the floor, curl up in the fetal position, and start wailing like a baby. Then when they come over to try to help you up, kick them in the balls. Then run like the wind.

COLLEGE IS NO LAUGHING MATTER

Insight from Jimmy Dore:

"Don't call your fraternities 'frats,' because you wouldn't call your country 'cunt.'"

"They didn't like me because I told them I was never in a frat, and I could have been if I had just held that egg in my ass eight seconds longer."

STUPID FRATERNITY PRANKS:

University of Missouri, Columbia: A sophomore has pleaded guilty for his part in a bizarre fraternity prank involving a barrel of opossums. An associate circuit judge placed the student on two years' unsupervised probation and ordered him to pay a $500 fine for illegal possession of wildlife.

California State University, Fresno: Nine students associated with Sigma Nu were detained under suspicion of kidnapping their vice president. Even though campus police treated the incident as an actual kidnapping, they later said it was a result of a bet.

80. You Love Your Frat but Hate Your Big Brother

Pledging can be tough. No sleep, hazing, losing your dignity as a human being . . . *blah blah blah*. But that's where your big brother comes in to play. Your big brother is the one brother who is supposed to help you out and protect you when all the other brothers are after your ass. But unfortunately, big brothers are like real brothers, you get what you get. And your big brother is a total douche.

The WTF Approach to Dealing with a Bad F*#!-ing Brother

➤ OPTION #1: *Tough It Out*

Do what he tells you to do and keep your mouth shut. If the other brothers find out you are being disrespectful to your own big, they will make your life hell! Play it cool until you're a full-fledged brother, then kick the shit out of him, spit on his face, and light him on fire.

➤ OPTION #2: *Scream Rape*

Tell other brothers that your big brother fondled you. Explain that he told you it was part of the pledging process and you need to obey. Then tell the brothers you are thinking about going public with it. They will be so horrified they will immediately kick his ass out of the fraternity. No one wants that kind of shit getting out. If they really don't have any reaction, then you are *definitely* pledging the wrong fraternity. Get out now!

> ### OPTION #3: *Kill Him*

Seriously dude, just do it. Drug him, take him to some deserted road, and run his ass over. You'll be doing the world a great justice.

NOTE: *WTF* will not be there to post bail.

FAMOUS BIG BROTHERS	
Ben Affleck	Casey Affleck
Owen Wilson	Luke Wilson
Alec Baldwin	Billy, Stephen, and Daniel Baldwin
Eng	Chang (Siamese twins)
Groucho Marx	Adamson, Joseph, Harpo, Chico, and sometimes Zeppo
Adolf Hitler	Alois Hitler
Ted Bundy	Al Bundy

81. You Lose Your Pledge Pin after a Night of Partying

Aside from torturous pledging rituals like being made to eat feces while on all fours singing the national anthem (do they still do that?), most of the time fraternities require you to wear a pledge pin so that everyone on campus knows exactly which frat is torturing you. The pledge pin is a big deal, and losing it can be cause for immediate elimination. Unfortunately, after a night of partying, you do just that.

The WTF Approach to Hiding Your F*#!-ing Stupidity

➤ OPTION #1: *Lie*

Immediately explain to the brothers that someone from another fraternity drugged you and stole your pin. Then help them plan the inevitable retaliatory strike. Who knows, this could be the start of a huge war between fraternities. Someone might even get hurt or killed—all because you lost your pin. LOL. Wouldn't that be a riot?

MOVIES SAY IT BEST

Peter: Doesn't it bother you that you have to get up in the morning and you have to put on a bunch of pieces of flair?

Joanna: Yeah, but I'm not about to go in and start taking money from the register.

Peter: Well, maybe you should. You know, the Nazis had pieces of flair that they made the Jews wear.

—*Office Space*

➤ OPTION #2: *Steal One of Your Pledge Brothers' Pins*

Pick the one that drinks the most. When he's passed out as usual, snatch his pin and, while you're at it, his wallet too. Buy yourself something nice on him. Fuck it.

➤ OPTION #3: *Quit*

Run away like you do from every problem, you despicable coward!

82. You Finally Move In to the Frat House and It's a Dump

After weeks of torture and hazing you have made it into the brotherhood. You can now sit back and enjoy all the perks of belonging to a fraternity, including living in the frat house. One problem though—the house is a total shit can! There is garbage everywhere, holes in the walls, mold on the ceiling, and fuzzy food in every corner of the house as well as what appears to be a human fetus on the couch. What's worse is that nobody seems to care. Sure you survived Hell Week, but will you survive living in this hellhole?

The WTF Approach to Living in F*#!-ing Filth

➤ OPTION #1: *Call in the Pros*

Hire a cleaning crew of hot, half-naked girls. Believe it or not, there is such a thing. Imagine: Hot girls in little French maid outfits, waxing your candlesticks. If every brother chips in a little cash, you'll be able to afford it—no guy is going to fight this one unless he's gay, in which case you'll probably find a way to throw him out of the frat. Once you see these girls on their hands and knees sucking up the dirt, it will all be worth it. Of course there'll probably be another mess to clean up after.

➤ OPTION #2: *Make the Pledges Do It*

Shit, that's what they're there for. They should be cleaning night and day. How else will they learn about brotherhood?

➤ OPTION #3: *Move*

If it's not required to live in the fraternity house, get your own place. Maybe you can room with another not-so-disgusting brother. Odds are you'll probably get laid more. No girl wants to screw you in a room with vomit in it.

➤ OPTION #4: *Deal with It*

You're in college for Christ's sake. Join the fun and stop being

a whiny pussy. Men are programmed to be slobs. And you want to be a man, don't you?

➤ OPTION #5: *Screw It*

Become an addict. If you're high 24/7 you won't give a shit about anything else. Careful not to overdose and die though—if the place really is a shit hole, they might never find your body.

➤ OPTION #6: *Get on* Extreme Makeover

Call ABC. Of course, they usually only help families who have suffered some traumatic event, or have gone out of their way to do good for others. So you might have to sponsor some poor, starving Ethiopian child. Or maybe tell them one of the brothers is dying and that his last wish is to see his fraternity house transformed. ABC loves that crap. However, if they do pick your house to makeover, you will have to deal with that annoying dipshit Ty Pennington.

WTF: UP CLOSE AND PERSONAL

My sister's room was always disgusting, but one month the stench was so bad that even she knew something was up. Every day it became more and more unbearable. Finally, she asked me to check her room out and see if that smell was "normal." It wasn't. In fact, I almost passed out instantly.

So she cleaned. And cleaned. And cleaned. Finally, she found the culprit of the unbearable smell under the bed: a badly decomposed bird.

Apparently, the cat dragged in a dead bird and put it under her bed. If you can imagine how gross a room has to be for someone not to notice an animal decomposing under their bed, then you have a clue to just how filthy my sister is. Sorry sis, 'tis the truth.

—GB

YOUR FRAT HOUSE MIGHT BE WORSE THAN A THIRD WORLD COUNTRY IF . . .

❑ There are more cigarette butts around the ashtray than in the ashtray.

❑ There are more maggots and roaches living there than brothers.

❑ You're starting to like the smell of urine.

❑ You or someone you know had a tapeworm in the last six months.

❑ You have an unexplainable rash spreading all over your body.

❑ The kitchen sink is sometimes used as a second toilet.

❑ You have fallen into a pool of semen.

83. Your Fraternity Is Caught Hazing Pledges

We all know the Greeks are known for their hazing of new pledges. But most of what happens is kept on the DL. However, every once and a while you get the one cry-baby pledge who runs to the dean and tattles on a fraternity. Now your frat is on probation while an investigation ensues.

The WTF Approach to Handling a F*#!-ing Hazing Charge

➤ **OPTION #1: *Deny It***

Unless there's a videotape, it's just his word against you and your bros. Assure the dean that your frat just partakes in harmless fun. Then kidnap the rat, tie him down, and force him to drink a mixture of lukewarm beer and hot piss.

➤ **OPTION #2: *Call in the Big Guns***

Most fraternities are national. Call in the national representatives to deal with the situation. You have better things to do, like beating the shit out of more pledges.

➤ **OPTION #3: *Change Your Ways***

Take the lead in publicly apologizing for the hazing that goes on at your frat. Become the John Kerry of fraternity pledging (we all know how well his outspokenness against the Vietnam War worked out for him!). Go around the country and preach about the dangers of hazing. Write a book, get on *Oprah*, and eventually get a show of your own. Then haze all of your guests.

> **NOTE:** *WTF* does not support or encourage hazing of any kind . . . unless, of course, it's really funny.

Cool Hazing Ideas

Make your pledge . . .

- Eat a bowl of cereal laced with thirty hits of LSD.
- Pull his own eyelashes out one at a time
- Listen to *Phantom of the Opera* or anything by Andrew Lloyd Webber over and over again
- Cut off his balls and eat them while humming "God Bless America"

Hazing in the Ivy League

Sometimes the spoiled rich kids haze their pledges in different ways from regular common folk.

Rich brothers in frats often make pledges:

- Drink white wine with meat in red sauce, and red wine with chicken in white sauce
- Register as a Democrat
- Suspend fencing lessons for up to a month
- Publicly reject the notion that Ronald Reagan won the Cold War
- Cancel their lifetime subscription to the J. Peterman catalog

for the ladies . . .

If by hazing you mean you circle the fat on your pledges, then please by all means continue. A lot of horny college guys depend on taking advantage of these emotionally damaged girls. Mess them up psychologically as much as you can so we can benefit!

Asian Student Hazing

Predominately Asian frats haze their pledges in slightly different ways than their Caucasian counterparts. Asian frats often coerce pledges to:

- Work on excruciatingly elementary and unchallenging math problems.
- Call their parents and tell them they don't want to study medicine anymore.
- Tell their ancient ancestors to go fuck themselves.

Hazing No-Nos

Hazing is an indelible part of the fraternity experience. But it can go too far. Avoid these techniques:

Water boarding: Now that a new administration is in office in Washington, you might actually get in trouble for this practice.

Crucifixions: While it would be a blast to make a pledge—crowned with a ring of thorns and carrying the crucifix on his back—walk to a desolate place as you lash him with a whip, it might make the pledge out to be a martyr if some of his close friends bear witness.

The rack: A trusty hazing tool since the Inquisition, the rack might not be as accepted by the campus police or local authorities as it was by the Catholic Church.

Burning at the Stake: This could get your fraternity a shitload of heat so don't even think about it.

MOST INTENSE HAZINGS IN HISTORY:

- Spanish Inquisition
- Salem Witch Hunts
- The Pogroms
- Armenian Genocide
- The Holocaust

> *COLLEGE KID QUOTE*
>
> **"**Me and the brothers once forced this kid to eat shit and then stab himself in the eye with an ice pick. That was so awesome!**"**
>
> —Danny Whackostein, junior at the University of Massachusetts

84. Your Little Brother Is a Total Loser

The fraternity had to take this little shit because he is a legacy, but unfortunately you were the one picked to be his big brother. You're supposed to help your little brother, but you can't stand him. WTF?

The WTF Approach to Ditching the F*#!-ing Dweeb

➤ STEP #1: *Make Him Quit*

You might have to take him, but that doesn't mean you have to like him. Give the go-ahead for all the brothers to make his life so miserable that he'll give up and quit, ruining his family name forever. Fuck him *and* his family.

➤ STEP #2: *Fix Him*

If he's a resilient little shit, do an extreme makeover on his ass. Just make sure he doesn't end up looking cooler than you. If he does, kick his ass.

SIGNS YOU ARE PLEDGING THE RIGHT FRATERNITY:

- Sobriety is seen as weakness.
- Wireless Internet server blocks everything *except* porn.
- Hazing involves being forced to go down on the head cheerleader for a grueling two hours.
- Tuesday-night poker was recently replaced with Tuesday-night freshman girls' oil wrestling.

Bonus Sorority WTF: You Wake Up with Your Underwear on Your Head

NOTE: This one's all for the ladies and does not directly apply to guys. But if you are a guy who regrets having sex with multiple women at a party, then you are an ungrateful son of a bitch.

You were having a good time as usual, flirting with the boys, pretending to be bisexual by making out with your sorority sister, and just being the overall drunk slut you've become since you started college. Everything was all good, and you were (sort of) in control. Until you took five shots of Jäger in a row. Before you knew it you were upstairs with a couple of guys and started taking your clothes off. And that's all you remember . . .

The WTF Approach to Piecing It F*#!-ing Together

➤ STEP #1: *Find Out What Happened*

Before you freak out, find out what happened and who you were with. Chances are that at least *one* of them wasn't as drugged out and drunk as you. Get the scoop.

➤STEP # 2: *Go to the Doctor*

If you don't remember using a rubber, go to a doctor and get checked out. You have to wait a month or two before finding out for sure if you're clear of a got-the-monster.

➤STEP #3: *Go to the Police*

If you think there was foul play involved, go to the campus police and tell them about it. We don't want to put a joke anywhere in this option—so continue to the next.

IF YOU JUST DON'T GIVE A F*#! ...

Now, if you're okay with doing three-somes with strangers and then black-ing out and not knowing exactly how you woke up with your panties on your face, more power to you. In fact, God Bless you—you make parties more fun. Make sure to blog about your wild experiences on your MySpace and Facebook page.

IN THE FUTURE . . .

Try not to drink so much and know your limit. Also, when you ask some-one what kind of pill they are offering you, don't take "it's blue" as a sufficient answer.

85. You Visit Another Chapter and They're a Bunch of Losers

One of the perks of belonging to a national fraternity is going to other schools to meet other brothers. And by meeting, we mean partying your ass off of course. So you and your brothers decide to take a road trip down to another school and crash at that chapter's frat house for the weekend. But as soon as you get there, you regret it. A lot. There are no old pizza boxes piled up in the garbage, no empty beer cans scattered on the floor, and no random passed out chicks wearing nothing but a big T-shirt. No, the house is spotless, the brothers are in their rooms studying, and classical music is playing just faintly enough to be audible. OMG, these brothers are a bunch of total losers! WTF?

The WTF Approach to Protecting Your F*#!-ing Frat's Name

➤ OPTION #1: *Stage an Intervention*

Sit these losers down and explain how a real fraternity is supposed to act. If they don't agree with your reasoning, throw a huge party and invite the hottest, naughtiest girls. Fill the place with booze and drugs and get down to business. Help them—they need you!

➤ OPTION #2: *Shut It Down*

Call the national chapter and have this frat closed down. Use any excuse you have to. You don't want these losers giving your fraternity a bad name, do you?

➤ OPTION #3: *Burn It Down*

Start a fire and let it burn. Sure it's tragic, but better to immortalize the fallen than cringe at the living.

➤ OPTION #4: *Take Advantage*

You drove all the way here; you might as well enjoy the weekend. Eat their food, sleep in their beds, and fuck their girls, if they have any. The truth is, you're considered their guests so have fun and let these nerds clean up after you.

COOLEST FRATERNITY NAMES:

- Beta Tappa Kegga
- I Eta Theta
- Alpha Cocks
- Busta Kappa In-yo-ass
- Beta Fucka Pussy and Drink Beer or Get the Fuck Out, Pussy!

LAMEST FRATERNITY NAMES:

- Beta Pi In-my-mouth
- Gamma No Hamma (Jewish Frat)
- Beta Gamma Rim-job
- Tappa My Ass
- Kappa My Balls

Chapter 9

Coed Anatomy 101

86. You Find Out That You Knocked Up Your Professor

You have been sleeping with your hot professor for a few months now and things are going great. It's a fantasy and a dream come true. Except that lately you've noticed something is different about her. She's been looking a little pale and fatigued, and seems to be getting sick to her stomach every morning. Is it a passing flu or something? No. Your professor is knocked up, and you're the goddamn baby-daddy!

The WTF Approach to Coping with a Big F*#!-ing Surprise

➤ OPTION #1: *Man Up*

You know what you have to do, so do it. Get a job, start a savings account, and offer your unconditional support. If that sounds like no fun, go to Option #2.

➤ OPTION #2: *Deny It*

If you really don't want anything to do with this whole situation, deny everything. If she wants to keep her reputation, she won't do much about it, except maybe fail you. It's not like she's going bring you on *Maury* and make you take a paternity test—unless she happens to teach a class called White Trash Studies.

➤ OPTION #3: *Abort!*

It's sad. It's difficult. But it's legal. Offer to pay for it if you feel that bad. Better to pay a couple hundred bucks than a couple hundred thousand raising a kid.

for the ladies ...

That would make absolutely no sense. Why the fuck did you even look here, dipshit?

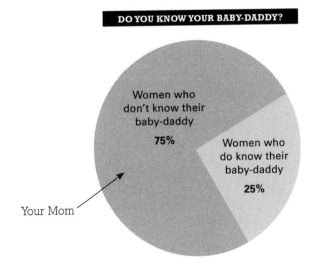

DO YOU KNOW YOUR BABY-DADDY?

Women who don't know their baby-daddy
75%

Women who do know their baby-daddy
25%

Your Mom

87. You Have Sex with the Dean's Daughter

Out of all the girls at all the parties in all the fraternities you had to take *her* home. She seemed like any other horny coed, and she was, with one exception—her last name. Turns out she's the dean's little girl, whorish as she may be. And the dean is one big, overprotective motherfucker.

The WTF Approach to Dealing with the F*#!-ing Dean

➤ OPTION #1: *Who Cares?*

So what? Why are you freaking out? He's the dean of a state university, not a mafia boss. Unless the school is in New Jersey, then he might actually be connected. If so, move to another state. After all, what are you doing in Jersey?

➤ OPTION #2: *Black Mail*

Screw her again, but this time get it on tape. This will come in handy, especially if your grades aren't so good. The last thing the dean wants is to have his little girl broadcast over the Internet giving a rim job. I'm sure there is some unclaimed scholarship he can give you—or maybe a rim job?

for the ladies ...

Of course this is undeniably hot, but screwing the dean's daughter is a bigger problem for you, since it also means the dean will find out she's a lesbian. Then again, that fact just gives you more ammo for blackmail.

88. You Run into Last Night's Hookup and Forget Her Name

You had an all-night sex-a-thon with some girl you met at a party. It was great, except you can't remember her name. No biggie, it's a big school; chances are you'll never see her again . . . until you run into her on campus the next day and can't remember her name. Shit!

The WTF Approach to Filling in the F*#!-ing Blanks

➤ **STEP #1:** *Deflect and Distract*

Use common phrases such as "Hey you" and then pray someone calls out her name while you're talking to her.

➤ **STEP #2:** *Go with a Nickname*

If the conversation goes any deeper, use a cute nickname like Bunny, Cutie pie, or Cuntie. She'll be so flattered that you like her enough to come up with a pet name just for her.

➤ **STEP #3:** *Be Slick*

To get to the bottom of it, make her put her name and number in your phone. This is a classic way to deal with not knowing a chick's name. Tell her how happy you are to run into her again then give her your phone and tell her to put in her digits. She'll include her name no doubt as well.

➤ **STEP #4:** *Be Direct*

When that doesn't work, knock her purse or backpack onto the floor.

Clumsily kick it around a little and pray that student ID or license falls out, then grab it, get her name, and give it back to her.

> **NOTE:** You and your friends should come up with a code word to use when you don't remember someone's name. Upon hearing it, your buddy will introduce himself and ask her name.

Slutty Girls' Names

You can tell if a girl will be easy by her name. Use this guide so you don't waste any time:

Heather: Big time ho name. Heathers are usually blonde and either really skinny or a little chunky with huge tits.

Christy: She's been with more guys than you want to know about. Wear two rubbers.

Veronica: Brown hair, big butt and tits, massive areolas. She likes to please and loves giving head.

Jennifer: This tall California blonde runs five a day, does yoga, and keeps in impeccable shape. She has a small, upturned nose, big blue eyes, and a rack to die for. She's a hottie, but she's also a fucking dumb bitch.

Melissa: Spoiled rotten and always gets her way, this chick will do you good, but it may cost you financially and emotionally more than it's worth.

Ellen: This is the kind of girl who lies in bed and does the *New York Times* crossword puzzle while you fuck her in the ass.

Sally: Lame, brown-haired Midwestern chick who might not put out right away but when she feels comfortable she'll turn the kink way up.

Anastasia: She's an unbelievably hot Russian chick with a body that could melt a cheese sandwich in Siberia. She'll be good to you, but if you cross her she'll stab you in the back . . . literally. Don't let her scowl throw you; Russians always look pissed.

Sharanda: This ebony princess is sexy beyond anything you could ever imagine and better in bed than every other chick you've been with combined. If you didn't vote for Obama, lie and say you did.

Emily: This sweet hometown girl loves her family and the church, but she also likes pleasing her man. Get in good with her and God and she'll do whatever you say.

Rebecca: Red hair, freckles (but not too many), big green eyes and legs that go up to her neck, this hottie smells like Irish Spring . . . everywhere. She'll do you after a couple pints of Guinness if you play your cards right. Refrain from asking if the "curtains match the drapes" if you want to score.

Tasha: White trash hood rat that probably got around as a teen. She is so sexualized that having sex is the only way she can express herself. Keeper!

Crystal, Daisy, Star, Candy, Bambi, Barbi, Lexxxi, Destiny, Savannah: Strippers. All of them.

Bobbi Jo: She loves riding four-wheelers almost as much as being on all fours. Bobbi could suck the chrome off of a trailer hitch. In fact, one time when she was so bored in her trailer, she did just that.

Buffy: Buffy loves playing tennis, wearing tennis skirts even when she isn't playing tennis, and taking frequent vacations to Jamaica where she "gets away from it all" ("all" meaning her stressful life as heiress) by getting ferociously gang-banged by hordes of angry natives.

Jodi: You wish. You could never get a chick this classy and hot!

for the ladies . . .

Who cares if you forget his name? Guys couldn't give a shit if you remember their names. Now, forgetting their cock? Well, that's just plain rude.

89. You Hook Up with the Girl of Your Dreams and Wet the Bed

You've been following this girl from party to party all over campus for three semesters (in this scenario, as in most of the ones in this book, you are a completely creepy loser). Finally, you get the courage to talk to her, thanks to your trusty pal, Jack Daniels. Luckily, she is also good friends with Jack, who convinces her it would be a great idea to go home with a loser like you. After engaging in mediocre but not totally embarrassing sloppy drunk sex, you awake to find that you have pissed all over yourself and the chick's bed. WTF?

The WTF Approach to Overcoming a Wet F*#!-ing Situation

➤ OPTION #1: *Get out!*

Grab your shit and take off. If she spots you on campus and confronts you, just deny it and tell her you left right after you came. Please, like you would ever spend the whole night with a tramp.

➤ OPTION #2: *Flip the Switch*

Quickly jump up and start blaming her. Be horrified and start to scream that she is a "pig" and a "gross fucking pee-ridden baby." After the outburst, calm down and suggest she go to a doctor because a grown woman wetting the bed is ridiculous. Then split.

➤ OPTION #3: *Own It*

Just admit it and tell her you wanted to give her something to remember you by. So you piss yourself sometimes when you're wasted. So what? Tell her she's lucky you didn't take a shit.

for the ladies . . .

Start giving head. We wouldn't notice if you had a dead body in the bed let alone a little bit of piss.

WTF: UP CLOSE AND PERSONAL

A good friend of mine (no I am not using this "friend" thing as a cover for myself—I've proved to be rather candid in this book, so you can trust me) was so wasted one night that he shat all over the kitchen (and himself) in his ex-girlfriend's apartment. Falling in and out of consciousness, he tried his best to dispose of the shit, but to no avail. Little tiny pieces of human doo-doo were scattered throughout kitchen and bedroom. The apartment looked like a friggin' guinea pig cage. (If you are reading this, I can't believe you did this. Seriously, bro!)

Turns out she sent him an e-mail the next day informing him that it "might not be a good idea to see each other anymore." Translation: you are a filthy animal and should be in prison.

Moral of the story: Don't shit where you eat . . . literally.

—GB

(But really GB's friend—seriously, I refuse to be connected with this violent and repulsive act! You're out there, buddy, and you know who you are.)

90. Your Roommate's Girl Wants to Screw You

You both met her at a party at the same time, and you always had a sneaking suspicion that she liked you. She laughs at everything you say, she holds on a little too long when you hug her goodbye, and once in a while she'll shoot you a look that sends a shiver down your spine and puts your cock in overdrive. These little flirtations were harmless, just good college fun. That is, until one night when she whispers in your ear, "I want to toss your fucking salad!" WTF?

The WTF Approach to Handling Your Roommate's Horny F*#!-ing Girl

➤ OPTION #1: *Do It*

This is college, okay? Turning down pussy is a big no-no. In fact, you could even say it is immoral.

➤ OPTION #2: *Just Say No*

If you happen to be governed by a different set of ethical principles (you are free to do as you please, though we strenuously object), then you might want to reconsider butt-fucking your roommate's girlfriend behind his back. Either keep your mouth shut or tell your roommate that his chick is after you. Then, take the first in a series of cold showers and cry like a baby for what you have given up.

HOW HOT IS SHE?

Since you can justify and rationalize whatever you decide to do (this is the beauty of being the shithead that you are), you might as well determine whether or not to face-fuck your roomie's girl according to how hot she is. Here's a hot scale to help you decide whether she's worth the trouble, with 1 being "maybe" and 10 being "fuck yes":

1. Hot enough to have sex with drunk
2. Hot enough to have sex with sober
3. Hot enough to masturbate to
4. Hot enough to masturbate to every night
5. So hot that you can't stop thinking about her
6. So hot that you get a hard-on just thinking about her
7. So hot that you'd give her a rim job if she wanted one
8. So hot that you'd beg her to let you give her a rim job
9. So hot that you'd let her pee on you
10. So hot that if you found out she had a dick you'd overlook it

COLLEGE TEN COLLEGE COMMANDMENTS:

I. Thou shalt NOT turn down good pussy . . . *ever.*
II. Thou shalt NOT study until the very last night before an exam.
III. Thou shalt eat shitty food and become a fat ass.
IV. Thou shalt remember thy pledge night and keep it holy.
V. Thou shalt NOT kill thy neighbor's beer.
VI. Thou shalt NOT date rape a chick that's passed out.
VII. Thou shalt NOT steal thy roommate's socks just because you can't find yours.
VIII. Thou shalt do as many mind-altering substances as humanly possible.
IX. Thou shalt NOT rat out thy neighbor unless he date raped that passed-out chick.
X. Thou shalt NOT covet thy neighbor's weed.

91. Everyone at School Knows You Have Herpes

We've all hooked up with that person we'll never forget, right? You know, the one that gave us herpes—the gift with purchase. Sure, it's a manageable STD, but there is no cure and it can be a deal breaker for some girls. It's all right though; it's your little secret. That is, until your roommate sees your Valtrex and tells everyone. Dick!

The WTF Approach to Being That F*#!-ing Guy

> **OPTION #1: *Admit It***

If everyone already knows you have it, don't try to hide it. The stress of lying will probably cause a breakout. Take your medication and be honest with the girls you hook up with. Girls are easy; if they like you a lot, they will forgive the seeping sores on your dick.

> **OPTION #2: *Share the Wealth***

Infect the whole campus, then it's no big deal. Find the few girls who don't know you have herpes and have sex with them. Then they will have sex with someone else and so on and so on. We promise that within a few months this will spread like . . . well, herpes.

➤ OPTION #3: *Get Even*

Pass it on to the dumb fuck who started this vicious albeit true rumor. Track down your roommate's girl and seduce her.

➤ OPTION #4: *Embrace It*

Stay home and play connect the dots.

WTFACT: One in four people between the ages of twenty-one and forty have herpes, so keep that in mind when you approach that group of girls at a bar.

WHAT THE F*#! IS UP WITH . . .
HERPES COMMERCIALS

Why do they always show people who take the herpes medication doing all these outdoor activities like eating ice cream, running on the beach, and skydiving? Could they not do these things before? Seriously, it's herpes, not spinal meningitis.

for the ladies . . .

If you have herpes, you're a dirty whore. Keep your legs shut!

POP QUIZ

Match the STD to the symptom.

1. Syphilis   **A.** Discharge from pee-pee
2. Chlamydia   **B.** Sores on your fucking dick
3. Herpes   **C.** Going blind and/or being from the nineteenth century
4. HPV   **D.** Burning sensation during urination
5. Crabs   **E.** Itching like a motherfucker
6. Gonorrhea   **F.** Being *anyone*

Answers: 1C, 2A, 3B, 4F, 5E, 6D

92. You Have the Smallest Pecker in Your Dorm

You knew you weren't going to be the biggest—the junior high locker room taught you that. But you definitely didn't think you would be the smallest. Certainly one of your twenty floor mates would have a smaller dick than yours. But just like junior high, your wiener is the tiniest—and everyone you share the communal bathroom with knows it.

The WTF Approach to Working with What You F*#!-ing Got

> ➤ OPTION #1: *Make It Your Thing*

Go out and make more African-American friends. Naturally you'll be the smallest among them, but they'll just figure it's a white thing and leave you alone.

> ➤ OPTION #2: *Get a Penile Implant*

You can increase your girth and length significantly for about $10,000. Take the school loans you were planning to use for living expenses and put it to your cock. Get a night job to make up for the financial loss. If you get big enough, you can do a little porn on the side to finance your studies.

> ➤ OPTION #3: *Buy a lot of Booze*

If you supply your buddies on the hall with booze and help them throw killer parties with a ton of chicks, they'll soon stop teasing you. You'll be known as the "big" guy (metaphorically speaking) in the dorm and maybe even on campus (if you buy *enough* drugs). Just don't get too whacked out yourself and start streaking again or you'll be back to square one.

➤ OPTION #4: *Be Smart*

Be the smartest and most academically successful kid on campus. At least some of your friends might have *brain* envy.

PROFESSOR TIP: In ancient Greece, an uncircumcised and small penis was seen as desirable in a man, whereas a bigger or circumcised penis was viewed as comical or grotesque, at least in intellectual circles. Too bad you don't have a time machine, huh?

WTFACT: LifeStyles Condoms conducted a study on penis size in order to ensure that properly sized condoms were available. During 2001 Spring Break in Cancun, 401 college students volunteered to be measured, of which 300 gained an erection to be clinically measured. The study found an average of 5.9 inches in length and an average of 5 inches in girth (circumference). How do *you* measure up?

IN THE FUTURE . . .

If you have a little pecker, don't let anyone know. Make up some religious excuse about modesty if your buddies want you to go streaking. In short, keep your little dick on the DL.

WTF: UP CLOSE AND PERSONAL

When I was at school, all my buddies knew that . . . wait, on second thought, never mind.

—GB

93. You Have a Reputation for Being a Player

Congratulations. Out of a student body of over 40,000 persons you've managed to develop a reputation as being the biggest man-slut on campus. But lately you find that your former exploits are starting to haunt you, especially when it comes to getting the really hot pristine chicks—girl-friend material. It seems that all the girls on campus are avoiding you because they've heard you're full of shit.

The WTF Approach to Playing the F*#!-ing Game

> ➤ OPTION #1: *Be More Persuasive*

If girls are rejecting your advances based on your reputation, you've got to up your game. Convince a girl that you really like her by saying things such as "it's different with you" and "I feel so comfortable with you, like I've known you forever." Then again, you probably already know how to bullshit if you're getting that much trim.

> ➤ OPTION #2: *Wear a Disguise*

Wear a fake mustache and talk in a foreign accent at parties. Hopefully the chicks won't notice you—at least until you disrobe.

> ➤ OPTION #3: *Keep Banging Hos*

Yes, it would be nice to get a nice, hot chick that could be a girlfriend, but those girls won't even look at you. Just keep banging sluts who like the fact that you are a player until a new class of freshman hotties who don't know you move in.

"Don't Hate the Playa, Hate the Game"

According to UrbanDictionary .com, here's the definition to "don't hate the playa, hate the game:"

Do not fault the successful participant in a flawed system; try instead to discern and rebuke that aspect of its organization which allows or encourages the behavior that has provoked your displeasure.

In other words, the individual is left completely off the hook, even

though his actions serve to perpetuate a corrupt or undesirable social system. Whew! This means you don't have to feel guilty about that sex tourism trip you planned to Thailand after graduation!

POP QUIZ

Match the "playa" with the "game."

1. Al Capone
2. Ulysses S. Grant
3. Albert Einstein
4. Henry Ford
5. Thomas Jefferson

A. The Civil War
B. Automobile industry
C. Banging slaves
D. Physics
E. Bootlegging

Answers: 1E, 2A, 3D, 4B, 5C

94. Your Sister Goes to Your College and Is a Huge Slut

If your sister was getting banged a lot in high school you would have been used to it by now. But back then she was a good girl and had the same boyfriend the whole time. Maybe it was the bad breakup after high school or maybe she just wanted to finally go crazy after years of teenage sainthood—whatever the cause, your little sister has developed a reputation for being the biggest slut on campus.

The WTF Approach to Being Related to a Lil' F*#!-ing Whore

➤ OPTION #1: *Change Your Name*

Choose a new last name and disown her. If you are Jewish, say the "Kaddish" (the prayer for the dead) and never talk to her again.

➤ OPTION #2: *Embrace It*

Be fair. If you like to sleep around, why shouldn't she? Come on, this is the twenty-first century so get a grip. So your little sister likes dick. So what?

➤ OPTION #3: *Blackmail Her*

Tell her you will tell Mommy and Daddy all about her campus exploits during Thanksgiving dinner if she doesn't pay up. If she's broke, get her to do your homework or write your papers for you.

➤ OPTION #4: *Transfer Schools*

Transfer to another school as far away as you can. You don't want to have to hear about your sister's slutty lifestyle from yet another frat boy. Make sure you transfer to a school in another state—she's probably slept with half the boys from other local colleges too.

➤ OPTION #5: *Talk to Her*

She may act like a two-bit skank, but she is your little sister after all. Talk to her and find out why she is acting out in this way. Some counseling and a pap smear would probably do her some good.

for the ladies . . .

If your sister is a slut, use it to your advantage. Find out who's good in bed and who's not. This way you don't have to be a slut like her just to get a good lay.

Ways to Spin Her Sluttiness

If someone says nasty things about your sister, spin it in ways that don't seem so bad:

Q: Heard your sister fucked two guys at a party last night?
A: My sister is a team player.

Q: Heard your sister likes to suck cock?
A: My sister is a skilled orator.

Q: Heard your sister likes to give rim jobs?
A: My sister is multilingual—she speaks many languages, including Greek.

IN THE FUTURE . . .

Don't go to the same school as your sister. The whole reason to go away to college is to escape your family, not to see them more often . . . especially if they're whores.

95. Your Sex Tape with That Freshman Girl Winds Up on the Net

You told her it would only be for your personal use, no one would ever see it. You even joked when she was a little reluctant: "It's not like it's going to be broadcast over the Internet or something." Then, somehow, some way, it was. WTF?!

The WTF Approach to Being a F*#!-ing Internet Porn Star

➤ **OPTION # 1: *Apologize***

Tell her you're sorry you turned her into a notorious slut. Then ask her if she wants to do it again, now that her dream of being the first woman president is probably over. See if she can have any of her remaining friends join in as well.

➤ **OPTION #2: *Don't Sweat It***

So what if your wiener is all over the Net? It's not like your mom is going to see your nasty little movie. (And if she does, ask her what the hell she was doing looking for porn!) Plus, with the grades that you're getting, it's not likely that you'll be running for public office anytime soon—unless you happen to be a Bush.

➤ **OPTION #3: *Start a Porn Website***

If your little video seems to be gaining some popularity on the web, maybe you should think about doing some more of these little films. Finance the rest of your college education by getting other impressionable freshman girls to make nasty vids. Focus on girls who are studying drama and tell them that you'll make them a star.

▶ OPTION #4: *Hide*

Lay low for a while in case your little starlet's father comes looking for you. Then again, she wouldn't be such a little slut if she had a daddy who cared. Put some time in at the school's gym just in case.

WHAT THE F*#! IS UP WITH . . . AMATEUR PORN

With websites like youporn.com and xtube.com, every average schlep can be a porn star. But who would want to see an amateur have sex anyway? You would never think to watch amateur football or baseball, so why would you want to watch some fat, sloppy loser with a five-inch penis perform pathetically average sex?

YOU MIGHT BE ADDICTED TO PORN IF . . .

- ❏ You spend more time looking for the "perfect" video to whack off to than you do looking for a girl to have sex with.
- ❏ The minute you cum, you check and see if there was a better video to jerk off to, which invariably leads to another in a series of masturbatory sessions.
- ❏ You argued with your Intro to Film professor that *Citizen Cum* was a better film than *Citizen Kane*.
- ❏ You actually pay for any type of porn.
- ❏ In your school papers, you keep misspelling "come" as "cum."

- ❏ When you ~~cum~~ come across a long free clip that buffers quickly, you know that your day just reached its peak.
- ❏ On a first date, you ask your new lady friend if she wants to have a threesome with the waitress.
- ❏ You take your girl to the petting zoo—and ask her to bang a goat.
- ❏ You believe the average penis length is a little over a foot.
- ❏ Every time your friend tells you about another great free porn site, you immediately cancel your weekend plans.

IF YOU CHECKED . . .

3–4: get a girlfriend

5–6: get a psychiatrist

7–10: get a priest

OUR POV ON POV PORN

POV–point of view—porn is really big now on the Internet (so we hear). POV porn is filmed from the perspective of the guy. The idea here is that it is apparently more erotic because it looks like you, the viewer, is the one receiving a blowjob. But can you really suspend reality enough to believe that you have a ten-inch black penis? And how come POV porn is only filmed from the perspective of the guy, what about POV porn for girls filmed from *their* perspective. Can you imagine? Just a big dick coming right for your eye . . . ahh!!!

IN THE FUTURE . . .

Never mind. No matter how this ends, making a porno with a freshman was definitely worth it.

96. You're a Senior and You Still Haven't Been Laid

Looking back, you don't know how it happened. One semester led to another, which led to another—and before you realized what a loser you were it was a month until graduation and the closest you had been to getting laid was that unenthusiastic hand job by that drunk freshman at that party—right before she threw up in your lap.

Are you hopeless? Probably. It was cute when you were a freshman, but now it's pathetic.

The WTF Approach to Getting F*#!-ing Laid

➤ OPTION #1: *Papers for Sex*

Obviously you're smart and studious or you wouldn't be such a sexless nerd. Even you dumb and ugly readers out there know that if you hang out at enough parties you'll get laid—maybe not by cheerleaders, but at least by the fat chick hovering over the cheese and crackers. So offer up your academic services to dumb broads that need to improve their grades. Write papers, tutor math, build science projects—use whatever expertise you have in exchange for a screw or two.

➤ OPTION #2: *Get an Ugly Freshman*

You're a senior now, and believe it or not, that impresses most freshman chicks. If you have to bang an ugly one for your first go, then do it. Beggars can't be choosers. A great way to meet these young willing girls is to buy beer for them, since they're underage. A couple six packs of Bud Light later and you could be getting your first blowjob. Drink up.

➤ OPTION #3: *Get a Hooker*

You've looked at craigslist ads every night for four years of college. You know that it only costs a hundred bucks for a half hour, but you just could never get yourself to go through with it and spend the dough. Desperate times call for desperate measures. So pay up and get it over with.

WTF ABOUT TOWN

After scouring college campuses around the country, we finally found a college student in his senior year who admits to still being a virgin. The following conversation ensued:

WTF?: So you are still a virgin?

Virgin: Yes.

WTF?: Ha ha, I'm telling everyone. Loser.

for the ladies . . .

Obviously if you are still a virgin now, it is a matter of choice. You're probably a very pious young lady. Don't give in to peer pressure, and stick to the high moral standard you set for yourself: giving blowjobs and taking it up the ass.

Chapter 10

Graduation

97. You're One of Ten Competing for Your Dream Internship

It's your senior year and it's time to prepare for life after college. You just found out that one of the best companies in your field is accepting applications for an internship position. This is just what you need, but when you go to drop off your resume, you find out there are at least ten other students from your school applying for the coveted position, many of whom are more qualified than you. Shit!

The WTF Approach to Securing the F*#!-ing Spot

➤ OPTION #1: *Flood the HR Department with Resumes*

Have you and your friends send in a ton of very impressive resumes under different names and then schedule a bunch of interviews, only to flake. This might convince them that a great resume isn't the most important thing in a candidate, giving you and your shitty one a shot if you can score the interview.

PROFESSOR TIP: If you get the interview, wear a suit with a power tie and look the guy or girl who is doing the hiring in the eye. Nobody knows how to interview people, and usually getting the position or not depends on bullshit like that. Also, read Dale Carnegie's *How to Make Friends and Influence People*. Maybe this will help you ace the interview. If nothing else, you can at least say that you read one book this semester.

➤ OPTION #2: *Lie*

We've told you this several times, and we cannot be more serious: nobody checks a resume! All they do at most is call your references. Get your friends Vinny and Joey to pretend to be whoever you want from whatever company you want. All they need to do is change their cell phone message for a couple days. This is not rocket science. Never let a bad resume stop you from applying to whatever job or internship you want.

➤ OPTION #3: *Come Clean*

Simply state your case. If you're an honest putz and there is nothing we can do to corrupt you, come clean in your cover letter that, while there may be more qualified candidates than you, it has been your dream since childhood to intern for a paper distribution company and you will do anything for this opportunity.

➤ OPTION #4: *Bribe Them*

Send gifts to secretaries and the HR people at the company—baked goods, bottles of wine, or a stripper if the internship is for a stockbroker trainee. Everyone knows stockbrokers love strip clubs.

DREAM INTERNSHIPS FOR COLLEGE STUDENTS:

- Medical marijuana tester
- Towel boy for girls' locker room
- Adult film reviewer
- Assistant to campus gynecologist
- *Girls Gone Wild* cameraman

WHAT THE F*#! IS UP WITH . . . FIRST JOBS

What is up with the fact that every job requires experience, even for an entry-level position? How the hell are you supposed to get experience if you need it to get a job in the first place? Even some internships say they prefer the candidate to have experience. It's a fucking internship! This is the Catch 22 of getting your first job—you need to have experience to get one, but you can't get experience without having a job. WTF?

98. You're Graduating with a Degree in Art History

It's a week till graduation and you're ready to get out there and make your way in the world. One problem: You have a degree in art history. So unless you are planning on becoming a professor or work in an art gallery, you're screwed.

The WTF Approach to Graduating with a F*#!-ing BS Degree

➤ **OPTION #1: Become a Famous Artist**

Even if you can only draw stick figures this can be accomplished. Art is subjective. Making it big has more to do with how you dress, where you hang out, and your personal mystique than it does the quality of your art. Remember, art history effectively ended with Andy Warhol and Pop Art, so there is nothing you can do that is new and interesting. Toss your cat in some paint, let him walk around on a canvas, sign your name, and hang it up somewhere in Manhattan with a $50,000 price tag. Rest assured, some jackass will buy it.

➤ **OPTION #2: Go Back to School**

Go back and get your masters. Then your PhD, then your postdoctoral. You'll be the most educated person you know. Sure, you'll still be a curator at the local museum, but at least you'll know your Monet from your Manet.

➤ OPTION #3: *Backpack through Europe*

Go to France, study art, bang some French girls, and eat croissants. The art degree will be very impressive over there. Europeans love useless shit.

CAREERS YOU CAN GET WITH A USELESS DEGREE:

- Pharmaceutical rep
- Bank teller
- Nurse
- Police officer
- Truck driver
- Legal assistant
- Bookkeeper
- Advertising salesperson
- Drug dealer

NOTE: If you have to resort to any of the above careers why did you go to college in the first place?

COLLEGE IS NO LAUGHING MATTER

"I have a friend who owns a Picasso painting. I'm ashamed to tell him it's been hanging upside down for nine years."
—Jackie Mason

99. You've Been in School for Six Years . . . and Counting

You never thought that you would actually end up being That Guy—the dude who spends eight years getting a four-year degree. But somewhere in between your first bong hit and the last class that you dropped, you lost six years. Six fucking years! And at this rate you still have at least another two left.

The WTF Approach to Being a Professional F*#!-ing Student

➤ **OPTION #1:** *Be Cool; Stay in School*

What's the rush? The economy sucks, work is horrible, and you'll never be able to get a girl to sleep with you for a case of beer ever again. If college is supposed to be the best time of your life, why not prolong it?

➤ **OPTION #2:** *Get the Fuck Out*

Get a prescription for Ritalin, overload your schedule, and take as many classes as you need to graduate. Stay up every night studying. With so many pill-popping all-nighters, you'll have at least finally lost the freshman fifteen you couldn't shake before (see "You Can't Lose the Freshman Fifteen" on page 22).

► OPTION #3: *Transfer*

Maybe it isn't you but it's the school that's keeping you unmotivated. Transfer to a school far away from your stupid friends and start fresh.

► OPTION #4: *Pose as a Professor*

You've been there forever and you're getting gray, you might as well use your distinguished looks to get laid.

YOU'RE TAKING TOO LONG TO GRADUATE IF . . .

❏ When you got to campus you joined the student organization: Abolitionists for Justice.
❏ Your first year tuition cost $25.
❏ You first studied the Depression in a class called Current Events.
❏ You'll never forget the day President Grover Cleveland came to speak on campus.
❏ Your orientation was interrupted by a Native American raid.

School Year Breakdown:

This is how you *should* spend your college years.

Freshman: Make friends with upperclassmen, learn to smoke pot if you don't already know how, and get laid as much as possible.

Sophomore: Torture freshmen just like you were, start throwing your own parties, and make a name for yourself on campus.

Junior: Pick a major, get a girlfriend, and get good grades to compensate for previous two years.

Senior: Bang every freshman chick you can, bang every freshman chick you can, and bang every freshman chick you can.

100. You're Graduating from a School No One Ever Heard Of

You finally graduated—and with honors—but unfortunately you went to Schmucks University somewhere in Schmucksville that no schmuck has ever heard of. You find yourself being asked the same question in job interviews over and over again when they read your resume. You went to school *where*? Where on Earth is that? Is that a four-year school?

The WTF Approach to Repping a F*#!-ing No-Name School

➤ OPTION #1: *Fudge It*

Say it's a private religious school. There are a ton of small private parochial colleges that are well rated but remain virtually unknown. Say it's the best school in the country for whatever you majored in. They'll never know.

➤ OPTION #2: *"It Was Free"*

Say you got a scholarship. If you say you got a full-ride scholarship, than you can't be blamed for going to some unknown shitty school. The best part of this lie is that it's virtually impossible for anyone to find out that you didn't get a scholarship, even if they did decide to check.

> **OPTION #3:** *Lie*

Again, we keep telling you to lie, so do it! Just say you went to Harvard or Yale. Nobody ever checks anyway. You can also audit a class at whatever prestigious university you live next to and legitimately say that you "attended" that college.

> **OPTION #4:** *Be Happy*

At least you didn't go to DeVry or some ridiculous school online. Right?

WTF ABOUT TOWN

WTF: So where did you go to school?

Loser: Joe's U.

WTF: Where?

Loser: Fuck you, bro. I'll write a book, you'll see!

WTF: UP CLOSE AND PERSONAL

I went to Hunter College, which is known in New York City as a pretty good school but is virtually unknown everywhere else in the country. So, how did I handle this? Well, I chose Option #3—I lied. Sometimes I'd tell people Harvard or Yale, and sometimes I'd be a little more modest and say NYU or the University of Chicago.

However, now that I have published five books and I'm basically better than you, I have to tell the truth (I can't start lying on the book jacket about my education). That's why today I just tell people that I went to NYU and then transferred to Hunter College because NYU was too expensive and I had to pay for it myself. This is also a lie, of course, but it's harder to prove. Well, it *was* anyway.

—GB

101. After Four Years of Partying—It's Time for the Real World

It's been a long, fun ride and one that you might have taken for granted. You learned a little, and partied a lot. Now it's time to graduate and get a job. Congratulations, welcome to the real world. It blows.

The WTF Approach to Life After F*#!-ing Graduating

➤ **OPTION #1: *Go Back to School***

That's right, stay a student as long as you can. People tend to expect less from you when you're a student. Don't disappoint them.

➤ **OPTION #2: *Deal with It***

We've all been there—that "what the fuck am I supposed to do now" feeling. Well, now you have a degree, so go get a job. (We mean when there actually *are* jobs out

there, that is.) You can always be the guy who's in his thirties but still goes to college parties. You'll probably get more action—or at least have money for better weed.

➤ **OPTION #3: *Join the Military***

Sure, the military is not like it used to be. You can't join the Reserves and putz around with guns every fourth weekend of the month. You'll end up in Iraq or Afghanistan. But at least you'll get to drive a tank to work instead of taking the subway. Commuting is such a drag.

for the ladies . . .

Do what you are expected to do. Get a job, marry some guy, and quit to take care of the baby. When he inevitably leaves you for a younger woman and splits town to avoid child support payments, go back to work and live a shitty life as a single mom. Better yet, sue your superior for sexual harassment and live off the settlement.

➤ OPTION #4: *Write a Book*

It served us well. We'll never do *real* work again.

➤ OPTION #5: *Kill Yourself*

We've suggested you off other people to get your point across, now it's time to turn on yourself. Take the hint. Hopefully if this book sells we can afford the lawsuit. Seriously, bro—do it!

➤ OPTION #6: *Take a Trip*

Search your soul and backpack through Europe, or better yet, somewhere cheaper and shittier. Make sure to write down what you mistakenly believe are interesting insights about the cultural differences in a little journal like every other backpacking piece of shit.

WORK IS NO LAUGHING MATTER

"My father taught me to work; he did not teach me to love it."—Abraham Lincoln

"I only go to work on days that don't end in a 'y.'"—Robert Paul

"A good rule of thumb is if you've made it to thirty-five and your job still requires you to wear a name tag, you've made a serious vocational error."—Dennis Miller

"I like work: it fascinates me. I can sit and look at it for hours."—Jerome K. Jerome

"The reason why worry kills more people than work is that more people worry than work."—Robert Frost

"Hard work never killed anybody, but why take a chance?"—Edgar Bergen

WTF?: College Final Exam

You've had plenty of practice with the Pop Quizzes—now it's time to take the real test.

MULTIPLE CHOICE

1. Two college students are partying like morons as usual. If College Student A slams five shots of Jäger and College Student B slams five shots of Jäger plus two Red Bulls, which student will be able to bang a girl before he pukes?

A. College Student A
B. College Student B

2. If you find small itchy bumps on and around your penis, you probably have . . .

A. Herpes
B. Crabs
C. Gonorrhea
D. Chlamydia
E. A lot of explaining to do

3. If you have an engorged penis, you might be . . .

A. Dying of syphilis
B. Dying of AIDS
C. Dying of Lou Gehrig's Disease—he *looked* like he had a big dick
D. Lucky

4. Which of the following females was the biggest whore?

A. Amelia Earhart
B. Queen Elizabeth
C. Cleopatra
D. Helen Keller
E. Your dead grandmother, may she rest in peace (even though she was a whore)

5. Which of the following is *not* a slang term for masturbation?

A. Punching the clown
B. Spunk the monk
C. Squeeze the cream
D. From the flesh Twinkie
E. Tug a Luggin

6. Which major is the easiest to excel in?

A. Chemistry
B. Biology
C. Psychology
D. Art History
E. Drama

TRUE OR FALSE

7. If your girlfriend goes on Spring Break without you, she is most likely a slut.

True   False

8. Your girl is most likely a slut anyway.

True   False

9. If you join your roommate for a threesome, you are gay.

True   False

10. If you join your roommate for a threesome and there are no girls, you are gay.

True   False

MORE MULTIPLE CHOICE

11. Where will two trains meet if Train A leaves Chicago heading east, traveling at 35 MPH and Train B leaves Washington, D.C. heading west, traveling at 45 MPH?

A. Who gives a fuck?
B. What are you a conductor? Why in God's name do they have questions like this?
C. What does this remotely have to do with real life?
D. You are too dumb to figure it out and therefore skip the question.
E. All of the above

12. How long is the average male erect penis according to a study conducted by Lifestyles condoms in Cancun during Spring Break 2001?

A. 9 inches

B. 12 inches

C. 5.9 inches

D. You are terrified to know the answer.

13. What organ will you most likely destroy in the next four years?

A. Liver

B. Heart

C. Brain

D. Testes

E. All of the above

14. Which of the following bio-logical phenomena occur during sexual intercourse?

A. Increase in heart rate

B. Increase in blood pressure

C. Cum and stuff

D. Laughter at the size of your dick

E. All of the above

15. What percentage of Americans believe that Creationism should be taught in schools?

A. 64%

B. 50%

C. 32%

D. 19%

E. 48%

16. What percentage of Americans obviously need *more* school?

A. 64%

B. 50%

C. 32%

D. 19%

E. 48%

MATCHING

17. Match the appropriate title in Column A with the appropriate person in Column B

Column A	Column B
1. Bad Ass	A. You
2. Pathetic Loser	B. Us

(feels like a real exam, doesn't it?)

18. How did the ancient Greeks take their meat?

A. Rare
B. Medium-rare
C. In their hairy, sweaty assholes

19. If you aren't ready to take a final exam, what should you do?

A. Wing it and take a chance
B. Stay home and lie, saying someone in your family died.
C. Drink Ipecac and vomit all over yourself and your classmates.

20. The German philosopher Fredrick Nietzsche famously proclaimed God to be:

A. Jewish
B. Vegetarian
C. Dead
D. Transsexual
E. An Underachiever

21. If your catch your roommate jerking off to hentai porn, you should . . .

A. Tell him later that it is impolite and for him to refrain from tugging on his chain while you're home.
B. Interrupt him and tell him to stop.
C. Wait and then interrupt him at the moment of climax by shouting, "Yes! Yes! Oh my God, yes!"
D. Start jerking off as well, and then have a heart-to-heart about how lucky you both are to have such a free and fun roommate relationship.

22. If you are hooking up with every girl in a three-girl dorm room, do you?

A. Have a foursome.
B. Proclaim yourself The Man until even *you* begin to tire of it.
C. Hook up with each one separately and play on their jealousy in a sadistic Machiavellian mind game.
D. Give them all HIV and leave town.

23. The 2009 Recession has been compared to the Great Depression. Which of the following is the biggest difference between the current downturn and that which followed the 1929 Stock Market crash?

A. Unemployment today is nowhere near Depression levels.

B. There aren't all those great bowler hats in the streets anymore.

C. Today, your grandfather is dead.

24. In general, Israel's policies toward the Palestinians are . . .

A. Fair

B. Unfair

C. Effective

D. Ineffective

E. You are an anti-Semite pig for even *thinking* about criticizing Israel.

25. Which of these is an example of a valid logical argument?

A. No vaginas are clean. Some vaginas are hairy. Therefore, vaginas should be avoided particularly during menstruation.

B. All sluts wear red. Your mom wears red. Therefore, your mom is a slut.

C. Some abortions are necessary. Some necessary things are fun. Therefore, some abortions are fun.

D. Some roommates are gay. All gays are you. Therefore, you are the gay roommate!

E. All sluts wear red. Your mom is a slut. Therefore, your mom wears red.

for the ladies . . .

26. What is the biggest bone in the human body?

A. Skull

B. Femur

C. Fibula

D. It varies depending on which basketball player you're dating.

27. In his *Republic*, Plato asserts that the best leader of the state would be a:

A. Philosopher
B. Lawyer
C. Economist
D. A black guy from Hawaii

28. If you throw up in a girl's lap at a party, you should.

A. Apologize and begin licking it off.
B. Change the subject by asking her what her major is.
C. Laugh maniacally as pieces of vomit continue to fall out of your mouth.

29. In Homer's war epic, *The Iliad*, Helen of Troy is said to have had a _____ that launched a thousand ships.

A. Face
B. Mole
C. Foot
D. Vulva

30. Which of the following is *not* a central theme of Buddhism?

A. Revere all sentient beings
B. Be one with the universe
C. Shove a gerbil up your ass like Richard Gere
D. Sit and say "Ohm" all day like a lazy jackass

31. Which of the following was *not* a cause of the War of 1812?

A. American expansionism
B. Trade tensions between Britain and the United States
C. War between Britain and Napoleonic France
D. Shit that was going down in 1813

32. Which of the following is *not* listed as a branch of government according to the Constitution of the United States?

A. Judicial
B. Legislative
C. Executive
D. FOX News

33. Which psychologist developed the theory of the unconscious?

A. Sigmund Freud
B. That other Jew, what's his name? Sounds like an Asian name. Not Freud. Um . . . Jung. That's right, Karl Jung.
C. Still some *other* Jew you can't remember
D. Dr. Phil

34. Which of the following is *not* an invention of the ancient Chinese?

A. Gun powder
B. Paper
C. Silk
D. Dry cleaning

35. Which of the following is true about the ancient Aztecs?

A. They built some of the largest and most architecturally complex pyramids in the world.
B. Their capital city of Tenochtitlan was bigger than any city in Europe at the time of its discovery by Spanish explorer and vicious murderer, Hernán Cortés.
C. They developed a really cool calendar.
D. They were blood thirsty, human sacrifice-obsessed pagans who had to be subdued and destroyed in the name of Christ Almighty.
E. All of the above

36. Which work of art best represents the process in which the artist "randomly" sprays his medium in a process known as dripping or splattering:

A. Jackson Pollock, *Number 31*
B. Hans Hoffman, *The Gate*
C. Helen Frankenthaler, *Mountains and Sea*
D. Peter North, *North Pole: The Loadman Commith*

37. If you are caught drinking liquor in class, you . . .

A. Smash the bottle in half, run up to the professor, and slice his throat.
B. Sing drinking songs so loud that you drown out your professor's complaints.

C. Say you are sorry and leave politely.

D. Shit on your desk because you are already in trouble and you might as well take the opportunity to do the one thing in your life you have always dreamed of doing.

38. In Herman Melville's epic novel, *Moby Dick*, Captain Ahab's relentless quest for the mysterious "White Whale" can be understood as a metaphor for:

A. Man's desire to control his fate

B. Man's desire to conquer God/Nature

C. 19th Century Imperialism

D. Man's love of boats

E. Jewish conspiracy to control the oceans and hence the world's seafood supply using deadly remote controlled robotic whales

FILL IN THE BLANKS

39. Word bank for the following sentences:

| *WTF? College* | talented | dead | tiny | pimples | dunce |

I wish I was as _____ as _____ authors Gregory
                         [A]   [B]

Bergman and Jodi Miller, but unfortunately I am a total _____.
                                                                          [C]

I have a lot of _____ and my penis is so embarrassingly
                           [D]

_____ that sometimes I wish that I were _____.
       [E]   [F]

40. How many times in this book has WTF used the word "cock"?

A. 25

B. 12

C. 2

D. Not enough

41. Which one has *not* been suggested as an option?

A. Blow up a building

B. Develop an eating disorder

C. Kill fellow athletes

D. Steal your roommates identity

E. Rape your mom

42. What option does *WTF* suggest you pursue the most?

A. Transfer schools

B. Kill your roommate

C. Kill yourself

D. Fake your own death

43. How many times has *WTF* suggested murder as a viable option for dealing with a difficult situation?

A. 10

B. 5

C. 7

D. 2

E. Too many to count

44. How many times has *WTF* suggested you kill yourself?

A. 4

B. 22

C. 5

D. 9

E. Seriously bro, do it!

45. How many times is AIDS used as the butt of a joke in this book?

A. 5

B. 15

C. Too many

D. Far too many that it's not even funny anymore and illustrates the authors' laziness, lack of creativity, and embarrassingly low literary standards. Seriously, how can they publish such crude dribble?

46. *WTF?: College* is the most interesting, provocative, and hysterical book ever written

A. True

B. Very true

EXTRA CREDIT: ESSAY CONTEST

Have any of the crazy situations in this book ever happened to *you*? In 500 words or less, describe your experience and how it has affected you. Check out WTFComedyStop.com for details on how to enter.

_____

_____

_____

_____

_____

_____

_____

_____

_____

_____

_____

_____

_____

_____

_____

_____

Answer Key

1. A (however, if College Student B does not throw up, the Red Bull will enable him to have sex with more gusto and concentration)

2. A or A & E (depending on whether you've got a girlfriend)

3. D

4. E

5. E

6. A or B if you're Asian; D or E for everyone else

7. True

8. True

9. False (if you keep your hands off his balls this is all just good clean American fun)

10. True—queer!

11. E

12. C or D (the only difference is that you are a pathetic loser if you chose D)

13. E

14. E

15. A

16. A

17. 1B, 2A

18. C

19. C

20. C

21. B

22. A

23. C (that's right, and Grandpa is never coming back—deal with it you weak little scum!)

24. D (unless you support Hamas, then E)

25. E (compare with B: it does not follow logically from "all sluts wear red" to "everyone who wears red is a slut." Thus, your mom can wear red and be a slut or wear red and not be a slut. However, chances are she's still a slut.)

26. D—yummy!

27. A

28. C

29. A

30. C (however, it is encouraged by some San Francisco sects)

31. D

32. D (and let's hope it stays that way)

33. A

34. D (one early inventor of dry cleaning was actually an African-American ex-slave, Thomas Jennings. He was the first black person in the U.S. to hold a patent. There is nothing funny about that and all African-Americans and dry-cleaners should pay homage to this great man.)

35. E

36. D (seriously, is that guy unreal or what? One day they'll put his cock in the Smithsonian.)

37. D (the logical thing to do is always the right thing to do. Remember that.)

38. E (read between the lines. You have to read between the lines.)

39. A-talented; B-*WTF?: College*; C-dunce; D-pimples; E-tiny; F-dead

40. D

41. E (what are we, animals? That is just plain wrong!)

42. A

43. E

44. E

45. D (a resounding *D*!)

46. B (if you got this one wrong, then fuck you!)

ART CREDITS